Lao Tzu and Confucius Meet Heisenberg

This highly original book offers a new philosophy and vision of higher purpose for leaders facing the immense challenges of the 21st century. By exploring Western quantum physics and traditional Chinese thought, leading management thinker Danah Zohar develops an emergent, new East/West vision that leads not just to global co-operation but to an exciting and revolutionary global co-creativity.

Taking complex ideas and presenting these in a highly engaging and readable way, this book offers the most recent thinking of Danah Zohar's quantum management theory. It demonstrates how the roots of this new philosophy and sense of higher purpose are both ancient and modern, drawn from traditional Chinese thought that had its beginnings thousands of years ago and from quantum physics, first discovered at the beginning of the 20th century. The new generation of quantum management is characterised by being more holistic, dynamic, and humanistic. Written in a very accessible way, Danah vividly demonstrates the advanced nature and scalability of quantum management by using real-world examples.

This book provides a foundation for a new leadership vision and style, based on moral renewal, greater cross-cultural understanding, and global harmony, and is truly thought-provoking for business leaders and management researchers.

Danah Zohar has been described by *The Financial Times* as "one of the world's 50 leading management thinkers" and has been elected to the Thinker's 50 Management Hall of Fame. She is the originator of Quantum Psychology, Quantum Social Theory, SQ: Spiritual Intelligence, and Quantum Management Theory, and the author of the best-selling *The Quantum Self* and *The Quantum Society*.

"I strongly recommend Danah Zohar's fluent and engaging *Lao Tzu and Confucius Meet Heisenberg*. In this new work addressed to non-specialist readers seeking to improve the management of their own organisations, she applies her long-term project of replacing the rigid mechanical hierarchies of Newtonian science with the dynamic creative flexibility of Quantum science. Her aims are to reconfigure our grasp of individual and collective human agency and to liberate and transform the patterns of leadership in the management of complex organisations. In doing so, she digs deeper into features of ancient Confucian and Daoist thought in China of the sort that actually helped to frame the methods and insights of great figures in modern Quantum science. Her work is practical as well as theoretical in that it records benefits gained by organisations like the Haier Corporation that have adopted her quantum management method to their own local circumstances."
Professor Nicholas Bunnin, *China Centre, University of Oxford*

"A brilliantly original fusion of ancient wisdom and modern science, *Lao Tzu and Confucius Meet Heisenberg* unpacks the paradoxes of leadership through the lens of quantum physics and Chinese philosophy. Thought-provoking, elegantly written, and deeply relevant to the complexities of modern leadership, and to navigating the uncertainties of today's world."
Kate Byrne, *Co-Founder of CARE360 and Host of* Women Advancing

"Danah Zohar has done something remarkable—she has merged ancient wisdom with modern science to create a revolutionary model for leadership. This book is a literal game-changer for anyone serious about the future of business, education, and the expansion of human creative potential. A quantum worldview is truly emerging!"
William Malek, *Co-Author of* Executing Your Strategy; *Principal, Strategy2Reality International*

"Danah Zohar, the insightful founder of Quantum Management, blends Eastern and Western thought by elaborating on the essence of quantum philosophy through a cross-temporal dialogue between ancient Chinese philosophers such as Lao Tzu and Confucius and the eminent quantum physicist Werner Heisenberg. In setting side-by-side the philosophical and scientific ideas of quantum physics and ancient China, she adds a new dimension to her original theory, as well as contributing to the modernization of corporate management. I wholeheartedly recommend this masterpiece of management philosophy to readers."
Chen Jin, *Professor of Innovation Management, Tsinghua University School of Economics and Management; Vice President, Chinese Society of Management Science*

Lao Tzu and Confucius Meet Heisenberg

Leadership Wisdom from Quantum Science and Chinese Philosophy

Danah Zohar

LONDON AND NEW YORK

Designed cover image: Katie-Ann Rose Wolf

First published 2026
by Routledge
4 Park Square, Milton Park, Abingdon, Oxon OX14 4RN

and by Routledge
605 Third Avenue, New York, NY 10158

Routledge is an imprint of the Taylor & Francis Group, an informa business

© 2026 Danah Zohar

The right of Danah Zohar to be identified as author of this work has been asserted in accordance with sections 77 and 78 of the Copyright, Designs and Patents Act 1988.

All rights reserved. No part of this book may be reprinted or reproduced or utilised in any form or by any electronic, mechanical, or other means, now known or hereafter invented, including photocopying and recording, or in any information storage or retrieval system, without permission in writing from the publishers.

Trademark notice: Product or corporate names may be trademarks or registered trademarks, and are used only for identification and explanation without intent to infringe.

British Library Cataloguing-in-Publication Data
A catalogue record for this book is available from the British Library

ISBN: 978-1-041-03313-4 (hbk)
ISBN: 978-1-041-03312-7 (pbk)
ISBN: 978-1-003-62326-7 (ebk)

DOI: 10.4324/9781003623267

Typeset in Sabon
by codeMantra

For Alan

Contents

Foreword   *xi*
Acknowledgements   *xiii*

Introduction: Two Paths to a New Leadership Paradigm   1

PART I
The Quantum/Chinese World   9

1 The Universe in Which Companies Are Operating   11
2 Companies as Part of the Living World   23
3 The Higher Meaning of Leadership & Companies   33
4 The Mind of the Leader   42

PART II
The Quantum/Chinese Leader   53

5 The Quantum Leader as a Modern Sage King   55
6 Twelve Principles of Quantum Leadership   63

PART III
China's Quantum Leaders   79

7 Zhang Ruimin: Haier's Philosopher CEO   81
8 Haier's RenDanHeyi Model: The Management Revolution That Emerged from the Philosophy   88

9	Zhu Haibin: Saving the World's Bees	98
10	Li Ling: Quantum Management for Schools	102
11	Liu Qing: Towards China's Knowledge & Innovation Economy	111
	Conclusion: The Challenges & Opportunities of Quantum Management	116
	Bibliography	*120*
	Index	*123*

Foreword

A Masterpiece of Management Philosophy Blending Eastern and Western Thought

In this book, Danah Zohar, the insightful founder of Quantum Management, elaborates on the essence of quantum philosophy through a cross-temporal dialogue between ancient Chinese philosophers such as Lao Tzu and Confucius (with a particular focus on Lao Tzu) and the eminent quantum physicist Werner Heisenberg. As one of the most revolutionary advancements in 20th-century physics, quantum science is making significant contributions to breakthroughs in scientific understanding, technological innovation, and the formation of future industries. The holistic, emergent, interactive, and open characteristics inherent in quantum science are driving humanity towards more robust philosophical perspectives, such as the integration view, systems view, and peace view. By interpreting the rich humanistic and scientific ideas of Lao Tzu and the classic work *I Ching*, Danah Zohar further proves that traditional Chinese philosophy not only provided important intellectual inspiration for the birth of quantum physics but also clarified an all-embracing new paradigm that gave rise to a radically new system of management philosophy.

In the nearly 10,000-year history of Chinese civilisation, Daoist thought, as represented by Lao Tzu and *I Ching*, is the most scientifically reflective philosophy in terms of its cosmological views, holistic perspectives, and emphasis on emergence, interaction, and openness. Thus, Chinese philosophy, particularly Daoism, aligns with quantum scientific perspectives and quantum philosophical views, contributing positively to the formation of Quantum Management thought. Danah Zohar explicitly stated in an article for *Tsinghua Management Review*, for which I serve as executive editor, that "Quantum Management is Modernised Chinese-Style Management." In this book, Danah Zohar goes a step further by quoting other ancient Chinese scholars like Confucius and modern Neo-Confucian philosophers such as Wang Yangming and Zhang Zai. She integrates their ethical and cosmological views – such as Confucius' concept of benevolence, Wang Yangming's view of innate moral knowledge, and Zhang Zai's intuitive insights that the universe and everything in it is made of energy and constituted by relationship – into the new epistemology of science. This enriches the quantum-like Chinese philosophical perspective, which had previously been focused primarily on Daoism.

Having completed the brilliant dialogue between Chinese philosophers and Western scientists, Danah Zohar further advances her original theory of Quantum Management. The new generation of Quantum Management is characterised by being more holistic, dynamic, and humanistic. Therefore, this book can be considered the latest upgrade of Danah Zohar's Quantum Management Theory. In the latter part of this book, she vividly demonstrates the advanced nature and scalability of Quantum Management by using real-world examples, such as Haier Group's revolutionary *Rendanheyi* model, as well as case studies of new Quantum Management practitioners like Zhu Haibin from Wanshicheng, outstanding educator Li Ling, and Liu Qing from NICE, the Yangtze River Delta National Technology Innovation Center, a remarkable platform for technology transfer.

As an innovative researcher, management philosophy scholar, and philosophy enthusiast, I wholeheartedly recommend this masterpiece by Danah Zohar to readers. I also extend my gratitude to Taylor Francis for their foresight in organising the publication of this book. I believe its publication will make a positive contribution to enriching and developing management philosophy and Chinese-style management, as well as improving the modernisation of corporate management in both China and the West. Furthermore, I am confident that by further integrating Neo-Confucian thought – returning to Confucianism and blending Eastern and Western philosophies – and by absorbing the philosophical and scientific ideas of India, we can form a more complete system of quantum philosophy. This will cultivate more outstanding leaders for all of humanity and continue to build new heights for human civilisation committed to the idea of "appreciating the beauty of each culture, sharing that beauty together, and uniting the world in harmony."

Chen Jin is the Vice President of the Chinese Society of Management Science and Professor at Tsinghua University's School of Economics and Management. He was recognised as one of the 50 most influential management thinkers in the world in 2021 and 2023.

Acknowledgements

I owe a large debt of gratitude to many for their inspiration and help with this book. My good friend Johnson Chang gave me the use of an apartment in his beautiful house in Suzhou, allowing me to have a home, a quiet place to write, and the opportunity to experience normal daily life in China. Professor Chen Jin, a Professor of Innovation Management at Tsinghua University, has a profound understanding of Quantum Management and has helped to further its academic recognition and acceptance. The opportunity to have many long, philosophical conversations with Chairman Zhang Ruimin, the founder and recently retired CEO of Haier, has been an honour, a joy, and an inspiration, and greatly deepened my understanding of Chinese philosophy's contribution to modern management theory. Long conversations about the *I Ching* with my son Alan, with whom I share a love for both quantum and Chinese philosophy, have also deepened my understanding of that complex and seminal book. And many conversations with Professor Nicholas Bunnin of the Oxford University China Centre have also been both a joy and a great help. My very warm and wonderful Chinese friends have made me feel welcome, at home, and cared for during my many long stays in China. The Chinese people themselves, warm, friendly, polite, and always helpful, have been a joy to live among. The simple joy they find in life, their spontaneous dancing in the streets and singing in the parks, lifts my heart!

Introduction
Two Paths to a New Leadership Paradigm

Many readers of this book may find its title quite curious. Why imagine a meeting between Lao Tzu and Confucius, perhaps the two greatest fathers of ancient Chinese philosophy, who lived in the 5th century B.C., and Werner Heisenberg, one of the founding fathers of 20th-century quantum physics? What could the three possibly have in common? What could they say to each other? But as we shall see in the pages that follow, both Lao Tzu and Confucius, and their fellow ancient Chinese philosophers, and modern quantum scientists and philosophers like Heisenberg, had a great deal in common. If we could tune into conversations between them, I believe we could gain valuable lessons about how to meet the very demanding challenges and exciting opportunities facing 21st-century leaders. Imagining those conversations is one purpose of this book.

Another of my purposes is to draw from this dialogue the fundamental outlines of a new, 21st-century, leadership vision and philosophy. Not philosophy as an abstract, academic pursuit, but rather, philosophy as an overall, all-embracing framework of understanding and a practical guide that provides leaders with a knowledge of the world of which they are a part, the role their actions and decisions play in it, and how to make those actions and decisions most effective and most beneficial.

Perhaps the first ever statement of just how important it is for leaders to be guided by a sound leadership philosophy was made by another ancient Chinese author, Sun Tzu, in his *The Art of War*, written between 475 and 221 B.C. during the Warring States period of China's Zhou Dynasty. Sun Tzu set out five cardinal principles of successful leadership, and the first of these was to "know your philosophy." Another was "to give those you lead a sense of higher purpose." A leader's philosophy, he argued, is what determines both the style and principles of his leadership. His sense of higher purpose inspires that leadership and all whom he leads.

In the many books I have written about Quantum Management and quantum leadership, I, too, have long argued that possession of a sound philosophy and a sense of higher purpose are necessary foundations for the art of intelligent leadership. And, indeed, this common stress on the importance to leaders of having both a philosophy and a sense of higher purpose is just one of the many uncanny similarities I have discovered between the principles and thinking of China's ancient philosophers and those that form the founding principles and discoveries of today's quantum sciences, from which I have drawn so much in my own work on Quantum Management. Such similarity was first revealed to me during the first of my many long visits to China.

In 2014, Zhang Ruimin, the founder, and at that time still CEO, of Haier, one of China's largest global companies, sent an email to me saying that my books on quantum philosophy and Quantum Management had played a key role in his design of the company's leadership and management transformation process, Haier's revolutionary *RenDanHeYi* Management Model. Mr Zhang invited me to visit Haier's headquarters in Qingdao to meet him and learn about *RenDanHeYi*. (More about that in later chapters!) After visiting Haier, I embarked on a month-long speaking tour that took me to many Chinese cities. Everywhere I spoke, people attending my lectures would exclaim, "What you say is so Chinese! Your books are so Chinese!" This wholly mystified me because, apart from one undergraduate course at university on "Philosophies of the East," I had no previous knowledge about Chinese thought or culture. But as such comments grew more frequent on my repeated visits to China, natural curiosity moved me to embark on the long study of the Chinese classics and Chinese culture that have led to my writing this book – and another of my purposes for doing so.

Because of the many how striking similarities revealed, reading the *I Ching* and the great books of Daoism, Confucianism, and Chan (Zen) Buddhism that laid the foundations of Chinese culture also led to my having a much deeper understanding of quantum science and quantum philosophy themselves, and I think readers of this book can benefit in the same way. Quantum physics can seem very abstract and unapproachable – frankly scary, to many. As we shall see, even quantum physicists themselves insist that it is impossible to *understand* quantum physics. By contrast, Chinese philosophy is very concrete and down-to-earth. It offers an easily grasped description of the universe we live in, how everyday human life relates to the wider universe, the role we humans play in this larger scheme of things, and thus the purpose of our being here. In clear, simple language, these Chinese classics tell us how to lead meaningful lives, how to be a good person, how to be a good leader, why and how to serve others, etc.

In its own often inscrutable way, the philosophy derived from quantum physics offers these same valuable insights. But by setting quantum science and Chinese philosophy side by side, by letting the likes of Lao Tzu and Confucius, and Heisenberg engage in conversation, these two very different and yet in many ways uncannily similar traditions strengthen each other, and their juxtaposition strengthens our understanding and appreciation, and the valuable lessons we can learn, from both.

In fact, just such a dialogue between the early discoveries of quantum physics and the lessons of Chinese philosophy played a key role in the development of quantum physics itself. Western scientists first looked to the Chinese classics for help in the early 1930s. The Danish physicist Niels Bohr was among the small group of pioneers who first tried to model and understand the "curious behaviour" of the quantum micro-world they had discovered within the atom. Like his colleagues Einstein, Dirac, Schrodinger, and Heisenberg, Bohr could not understand the results of experiments that indicated light sometimes behaved like a stream of particles but under other circumstances seemed to be a series of waves. According to Western logic and intuition, light should be *either* particle-like, *or* wave-like, because nothing can ever be *both* "this," *and* its opposite, "that." In the West, something is always *either* black *or* white, true *or* false, good *or* bad, etc., and yet light seemed to be *both* particle-like *and* wave-like – and at the same time! "How could this be possible?!" Bohr wondered. Faced with similar logic-defying mysteries about the new quantum science they were discovering, Einstein called it "Alice-in-Wonderland physics! Schizophrenic physics!", and until the end of his life could never fully accept it. But Bohr decided to look outside the Western tradition for some understanding.

Like his fellow physicist Wolfgang Pauli, Bohr had become interested in ancient Chinese philosophy, and was familiar with the *I Ching*. Turning to the *yin/yang* dynamic and the notion of *complementary* opposites that form the structure of the *I Ching* and then continue through Chinese thought ever after, Bohr could see a possible model for quantum "wave/particle duality," and a different kind of logic that could grasp *both/and* pairs of apparent opposites. Reasoning that, just like *yin* and *yang*, the wave-like and particle-like nature of light could be two aspects of one dynamically moving, recurrent process, Bohr was able to publish his famous Principle of Complementarity, one of the building blocks of the new quantum physics. Heisenberg quickly followed this lead and argued that other mysterious pairs of seemingly complementary opposites, like *position* and *momentum*, *spin-up* and *spin-down*, might be understood in the same way. Like Bohr, he concluded that, though only one member of these complementary opposites could ever be observed at any one time, both were necessary to understand the underlying nature of the quantum phenomenon in question. This was published as Heisenberg's Uncertainty Principle, another fundamental building block of the new physics.

Through this helpful influence on Bohr and Heisenberg's thinking, ancient China had made its first contribution to what would become the 20th century's revolutionary quantum physics. As a token of recognition, and of his gratitude, Bohr had the famous Daoist *yin/yang* symbol engraved on his personal Coat of Arms. A further Chinese contribution was made through the later, ground-breaking, work of David Bohm, who did the foundational work on solid-state physics, observed the first evidence for the existence of quantum non-locality (the Bohm-Aharonov Effect), and put forward one of the leading interpretations of the "Observer Effect" in quantum theory. Bohm had been strongly influenced in his thinking by the philosophies of Spinoza and Alfred North Whitehead, both of whom were themselves strongly influenced by traditional Chinese thought. As a result, much of Bohm's own thinking about quantum physics was very "Chinese." And David Bohm was the greatest influence on my own lifelong interest in quantum physics and the wider philosophical implications I have tried to tease out from within it. I first discovered quantum physics at the age of 15 by reading his classic textbook, *Quantum Theory*, and for the final ten years of Bohm's life, I enjoyed his close personal friendship and mentoring.

So, while 20th-century Western scientists did the first actual experiments that discovered modern quantum physics, and were the ones who formulated the equations that made further experiments and technological applications possible, most insist even to this day that it is impossible to *understand* quantum physics. It is "illogical," "counter-intuitive," and "irrational" they claim. Noble scientist Richard Feynman famously said, "If you think you understand quantum physics, then you don't!" But I shall argue in this book that, in many ways, the Chinese have thought in a quantum way, and had an intuitive grasp of quantum logic and quantum reality, for over 3000 years, and that modern Western science has only just caught up with what the Chinese have known since early antiquity. Thus, it is my hope that reading this book will help more Western people "make sense" of quantum physics.

We will see that many of the philosophical insights and leadership lessons first presented in the *I Ching*, and those of thinkers like Lao Tzu, Zhuangzi, Confucius, Mencius, Zhang Zai, and Wang Yangming, based on their intuitive understanding of the universe, were an uncanny prevision of later scientific facts discovered through experiment by scientists exploring quantum physics and quantum field theory and of the leadership lessons that form the basis of my own Quantum Management Theory. Indeed, I believe that quantum physics and its sibling, complexity science, have simply given important strands of traditional Chinese thought experimental verification and expressed them in equations. Thus, in some important ways, the Chinese can rightly claim to have invented quantum thinking, and to enter into much of Chinese thought is to understand the principles of quantum physics. I also believe that to practice quantum thinking in business is, in some important ways, to do business in a characteristically Chinese way. I even want to suggest that Quantum Management could be offered as modernised Chinese management and quantum thinking as modernised Chinese thinking. Many Chinese companies today are, in fact, describing themselves as quantum companies.

But in suggesting this and in describing all the many commonalities between early Chinese thought, quantum thinking, and Quantum Management, it is equally important to mention many very important differences. China is a very old society, and its culture is extremely complex. Chinese thought is certainly not monolithic. Alongside Lao Tzu's famous *wu wei*, or "hands off" philosophy of no control, no interference, and Wang Yangming's *Liangzhi*, a faith that every individual possess the moral intuition to know right from wrong and thus an inviolable personal authority in his own right, sits the mainstream Confucian tradition's faith in the unquestionable authority of the ruler and the father, and the critical role of social rituals and social propriety to control the people's baser instincts and ensure their moral cultivation. And this Confucian influence has meant that traditional Chinese management has always emphasised autocratic and paternalistic leadership, central control, and hierarchy – all things rejected by Quantum Management. Yet at the same time, Confucius himself advocates asking many questions, respecting the independent authority of the craftsman or a lower official who does his job competently, and argues that the ruler should listen attentively to those who disagree with him and "consider many points of view."

And alongside its non-quantum liking for authority and control, traditional Chinese management also stresses the importance of strategic flexibility, adapting to changing circumstances, and spontaneity – all things advocated by Quantum Management. Both the very Confucian traditional Chinese management and Quantum Management stress virtue, wisdom, and learning as necessary qualities of the leader, and both stress the power and importance of relationships, trust, and shared values. Some Confucian values are very non-quantum, others more so. And Confucianism itself is dynamic and changing and subject to many interpretations. I think important leadership lessons can be learned from both the similarities and differences, and thus a conversation between Confucius and Heisenberg can be as instructive as one between Heisenberg and Lao Tzu, Zhangzu, or Wang Yangming.

And just as I believe a deep Chinese understanding of quantum thinking, and its rich expression throughout many strands of Chinese culture, even to this day, could lead Western scientists to better understand what they have themselves now discovered, the very concrete and quantum-like leadership wisdom outlined by the Chinese can offer Western leaders a more solid foundation for practising Quantum Management principles. And seeing the Chinese and quantum systems of thought set side by side can help Western people in general better understand that Western logic and the Western way of thinking are not the *only* kind of logic and thinking, and perhaps not even always the *best* kind for adjusting to the challenges of life in the 21st century.

Both quantum physics and much of Chinese thought make the Western person confront himself, question himself, and doubt himself. Such self-questioning and self-doubt can be creative, opening the mind to new ways of thinking. Describing how the ancient Chinese very early on passed through the stages of a male-dominated monotheism, a dualism that divides reality into separate spheres of mind, or spirit, and matter, and a belief that man is separate from nature and the cosmos, the translator and author David Hinton has written that the Chinese model is particularly relevant to our own contemporary situation and challenges. "China was almost three thousand years ahead of the West in this regard," he writes, "and their innovations present a radical alternative to our culture's traditional assumptions."[1]

Were the West to gain this insight, and to acquire the cultural humility that would accompany it, much would be gained for better global understanding and world peace. It would certainly offer a greater understanding of many features of today's China and contribute to a more positive East/West dialogue that would benefit all. At the same time, seeing how closely elements of their own tradition are reflected in the discoveries, thinking, and language of today's best science may assure the Chinese they need not always or only adopt Western ways to be modern. In fact, the synergy between the new quantum thinking, and thus an ability to *understand* quantum physics, and the way many Chinese have always thought, may confer great technological advantage for China. Many Chinese scientists are "at home" with this physics, and its technological implications come naturally to them. And finally, through this dialogue between Western quantum physics and elements of traditional Chinese thought, we might even arrive at an emergent, new East/West vision leading not just to global cooperation but to exciting and revolutionary global co-creativity. To gain a knowledge of Chinese Daoist and Neo-Confucian thought, and see its expression alongside the more scientific language of quantum physics, is to gain the foundation for a truly contemporary, global modernity.

While I hope my overall theme of the similarities between much of the traditional Chinese worldview and the quantum worldview is of general interest, in what follows I will be concentrating on the common leadership ethos, principles, and philosophy arising from both, and addressing myself primarily to leaders in the business world. I believe that everything that follows has management implications, and I shall do my best to bring these to readers' attention as I write.

This book, then, can also be seen as a deeper philosophical and historical accompaniment to my earlier books on quantum leadership and Quantum Management Theory. It offers some of that "deep stuff," a grasp of which distinguishes a great leader from a good manager. The practical, nuts and bolts implementation of Quantum Management principles calls upon companies to end top-down control, rid themselves of bureaucracy, and replace these with a network of well-connected and co-creative, self-organising autonomous teams functioning as a holistic ecosystem. But these practical principles are embedded within a wider, new philosophical framework that both inspires and facilitates them and that gives Quantum Management a higher, indeed even spiritual, dimension. This philosophical side of Quantum Management, like much of Chinese philosophy itself, calls upon us (*especially* those of us in the Western world!) to rethink really deep questions about the nature and purpose of our human lives and leadership, our place, and that of our companies, in the cosmos and the realm of nature as well as wider society, the nature of consciousness and the capacities of the human mind, and the very nature of our thought. We will see that all of these bear on the qualities desired in a great leader.

Part III of this book concludes that Quantum Management can be thought of as modernised Chinese management. To support this, it offers profiles of, and interviews with, various contemporary Chinese leaders in business and education whose leadership philosophy and practice have been inspired by their knowledge of traditional Chinese philosophy and of ideas from quantum science. Foremost among these leaders interviewed is Zhang Ruimin, Chairman of the Haier Group, whose RenDanHeYi Management Model was the first practical, and in my view most effective and thorough, business model to implement the principles of Quantum Management in daily organisation and practice. The self-declared Quantum Management practices of other Chinese companies are pretty much variations of the RenDanHeYi Model. Throughout this book, I will refer to RenDanHeYi as a *generic* guide for implementing Quantum Management in companies. Haier was the first to conceive the RenDanHeYi Model, but as Zhang Ruimin himself has said, it now belongs to all. Haier has its own way of practising RenDanHeYi, but other companies can now find *their* way of doing so.

Finally, I must add an important note of explanation and caution to readers and to those who might be tempted to criticise all references to "quantum" in this book. Quantum physics itself, of course, has nothing to say about the meaning of life, the qualities of good leadership, how to manage companies, nor much of anything else that would interest us as we go about our daily lives. It is a rigorous science expressed in formal mathematical equations that initially described the behaviour of very small particles found within the atom, and these equations allow physicists to make predictions that have practical applications in the laboratory and in the design of quantum technologies like computers, smart machines, the Internet, lasers, MRI scans, new materials, and artificial intelligence – all the things that define life in the 21st century. And quantum field theory, the most complex and thorough extension of quantum mechanics, has given scientists a much better understanding of the origins and nature of the cosmos. But the insights of quantum field theory, too, are expressed as even more obscure, formal equations and themselves tell us little of interest about the role or place of human beings in the universe. However, the deeper and wider philosophical, and even scientific, implications of that restricted focus of quantum physics as a science *have* been explored by quantum physicists themselves, by scientists working in other fields such as complexity science, quantum biology, materials science, cognitive science, and by philosophers with a background in physics like myself. And the defining principles and discoveries of quantum physics not only offer a new scientific paradigm but also clarify a new paradigm that has been emerging since the late 19th century throughout Western culture for rethinking our understanding of every aspect of our daily lives and activities. My own work, which explores this new "quantum paradigm," published in 11 previous books, has been devoted to exploring these wider implications of quantum science for new thinking about the nature and potentialities of quantum mind, quantum thinking, human psychology, social theory, management theory, and an over-arching new philosophy of life. Thus, the quantum philosophy presented in this book, though shared by many others, is drawn from my own personal understanding and from the strong influence on my thinking of David Bohm's work – and turns out, in many ways, to be very Chinese! The still wider, ongoing discoveries and applications based on the defining principles of quantum physics continue to revolutionise both our understanding and the material conditions of our daily lives. As Professor Vlatko Vedral of Oxford University wrote in *Scientific American*, "We live in a quantum world."[2] And were he alive today, Lao Tzu might add, "I told you so!"

Notes

1 David Hinton, *China Roots*, 11.
2 *Scientific American*, June 2011.

Part I
The Quantum/Chinese World

1 The Universe in Which Companies Are Operating

The Chinese *I Ching*, or *Book of Changes*, tells us,

> Here it is shown that the way to success lies in apprehending and giving actuality to the Way (the *Dao*) of the universe which, as a law running through end and beginning, brings about all phenomena in time.

And yet the leaders of human organisations seldom, if ever, give any thought to looking to the way of the universe when thinking how best to lead those organisations.

Recently, I was invited to give a Quantum Management workshop to a group of senior leaders from British energy companies. The companies represented were still drawing their power sources from fossil fuels. It was part of my speaking brief to raise these leaders' awareness of the role companies play in the wider scheme of things and especially to make them more aware of their own roles and responsibilities with respect to climate change. The men present were hostile and defensive. When I spoke about environmental protection, they responded, "The environment is the government's responsibility. Our responsibility is to meet our customers' demands and to make a profit from doing so." When I suggested they seemed unaware of what was going on just outside the window, they snapped back, "No, we don't know what's outside the window and we don't care! Our job is in here." And when I suggested their thinking was coloured by an outdated picture of man's relation to the universe and the world of living nature, a particularly belligerent man snapped, "I don't think we need to know all this deep stuff to run our companies successfully." But I believe "the deep stuff" plays an essential role in both the nature and thinking of leadership, and that deep stuff certainly requires an awareness of and a relationship to "what's outside the window."

These British energy leaders were, of course, citizens of the Western world, and they relied on standard Western management principles to govern their companies. Were they more aware of the "deep stuff," they would have known that their cultural background and traditional management practices had embedded a whole array of assumptions in their thinking that directly affected both their leadership attitudes and their daily management decisions and that these, largely unconscious, assumptions were dangerously outdated. Unwittingly, they were leading 21st-century companies with a 17th-century mindset. The management practices they followed had been advocated by Frederick Taylor, a Scottish engineer, in a paper he published on "Scientific Management" in 1911. Taylor's argument that companies are better managed if they follow scientific principles was sound enough, but the science from which he drew his principles was Isaac Newton's 17th-century mechanistic physics and from all the assumptions that accompanied that physics.

Newton saw the universe as a giant machine. It was simple, law-abiding (deterministic), and predictable; human beings were unique and wholly separated from both Nature and the cosmos; human beings were privileged and Nature was a resource for our exploitation; just as the cosmos was structured hierarchically, human beings were naturally sorted into a hierarchy of potentials, roles, and functions – and the higher should govern the lower. All these became assumptions built into the management of a Taylorian company. Just as Newton saw the universe as a giant machine made up of separate atomistic bits, so Taylor urged that the organisation should function as a well-oiled machine, divided into atomistic, separate, functional "divisions" organised hierarchically and controlled from the top with well-defined bureaucratic rules. Managers should manage and workers should do as they are told. As with any good machine, above all else, the primary value to be stressed was *efficiency*.

But in the early 20th century, Newton's physics was replaced by quantum physics, and a new theory of how the universe works and of what it is made. Entangled quanta of energy replaced Newton's isolated and material atoms. Heisenberg's Uncertainty Principle replaced Newtonian determinism. Simplicity and stability were replaced by complexity and dynamic, constant change. The separateness of the human observer was replaced by a participatory universe in which the observer and the observed were a co-creative unity. Quantum physics showed that human beings were not separate from Nature and the universe after all. Instead, our questions, our observations, our experiments, and our decisions play an active role in *making* the world – something we now realise all too clearly from our destructive role in climate change. And the later discoveries of quantum science's offspring, complexity science and quantum biology, have demonstrated that we human beings are living quantum systems ("complex adaptive systems") – made of the same stuff (energy) that everything else in the universe is made, and our "stuff" organised and acting according to the same principles as all life on Earth, both plants and animals. Quantum physics has thus given rise to a new paradigm that replaces that which arose from Newton's physics, and this new, quantum paradigm calls upon us to rethink everything, including the management of companies and the desirable personal qualities of the men and women who lead them.

I have published several books on Quantum Management as a more contemporary model for scientific management. Like Taylor, I argue that companies run most effectively if they are managed according to scientific principles, but I argue that the science from which these principles should be derived is today's quantum science. And from what I have just written, we can see that quantum science offers a radically different framework for understanding the nature of the universe, the nature of the living world, and the human relationship to each. All this has implications for the meaning and purpose of companies and for knowing the best way to manage them. A leader following the principles of Quantum Management will be basing his strategies and decisions on a very different set of assumptions that underpin the new quantum paradigm. And we will see that these are remarkably similar to the defining principles of much traditional Chinese thought and to the assumptions that frame the Chinese worldview, even today.

Like today's quantum science, the Chinese have always believed there is an intimate, defining relationship between "Heaven," the realm of larger cosmic reality and nature, and our human world here below. This relationship decrees that the Way of Heaven is the Way of Man – that we should look to nature and the cosmos for directions on how to govern and live here on Earth. The classic *Doctrine of the Mean* tells us, "What heaven decrees is called 'the natural'; to follow the natural is called the Way, to cultivate the Way is called 'instruction.'" (Note: The more imperialist mainstream Confucians who wrote commentaries on the *The Doctrine of the Mean,* interpreted 'heaven' as referring the Emperor, 'the son of Heaven,' but many commentators since interpret 'heaven' as meaning 'the cosmos.')

Thus, knowing what these two sister systems of thought say about the nature of the universe has direct lessons for leaders and the desired nature of the organisations they lead. In these next few chapters, I will tease out how quantum science and Chinese thought describe the nature of the world we live in, our relationship to it, and the leadership lessons to be found in this. Let us begin with the nature of the universe.

- *In the beginning...*
    All the cosmic origin stories in all the world's great mythologies tell of a primal, formless emptiness out of which our universe arose. In the Judeo-Christian *Bible*, it is described as a "dark emptiness." The Greeks referred to it as "dark chaos." In the *Tao te Ching*, we read of a *Tao* that cannot be named, a perennial Absence in whose relationship to Presence we find "dark-enigma within dark-enigma ... gateway to all mystery." Other Chinese writings refer to this Absence, or dark-enigma, as The Great Emptiness, *Taixu*, a formless Nothingness out of which all Being arises. In a further chapter of the *Tao te Ching,* Lao Tzu refers to this originating Absence as The One, and explains the sequence of creation as, "The one gives birth to the two, the two gives birth to the three, and the three

gives birth to the ten thousand things." The two, we are told by one later Confucian interpretation, was the Yang/Yin dynamic, a dialogue between movement and stillness, and the three was what the Chinese call The Five Movements, or the Five Elements. And the 10,000 things were all the many things that exist in the universe, things that can be seen, weighed, touched, and measured, including our human selves and our companies.

Today's cosmic origin story is, of course, told by science, by quantum physics and quantum cosmology, but this scientific account is uncannily similar to those of ancient mythology – and most uncannily similar to the early Chinese account. According to quantum science, the first thing to result after the Big Bang was the Quantum Vacuum, an unperturbed, dark field of pure, *still* energy without form and therefore without visible characteristics. This originating, still, quantum "One" then experienced excitation, a ripple of movement ("two") upon the still sea of background energy, and this gave rise to several more excitations, the Four Fundamental Forces ("three") – out of which all existing things have been born and bound into relationship. But the equations and experiments of modern physics allow us to shed more light on what the *Tao te Ching* described as that "dark-enigma within dark-enigma" – the nature of the Quantum Vacuum itself and the relationship of that originating "emptiness" to ourselves and to everything that makes the world around us. This scientific knowledge also reveals how close early Chinese understanding of these same things was to what quantum physics tells us today, and what both can tell us about something of great importance to companies.

- *The Hidden and the Seen ... Potentiality and Actuality*

Both the Quantum Vacuum and the Great Emptiness are named in a misleading way, because neither is actually empty. Ultimately, there is no such thing as true emptiness in our universe. The Neo-Confucian philosopher Zhang Zai spoke of "the fullness of utmost emptiness" and described it, rather, as being "undifferentiated." In the language of quantum physics, the Quantum Vacuum is filled with *potentiality* – the potentiality for everything that ever has, does now, or ever will exist. But potentiality cannot be seen, it cannot be described (i.e. "The Tao that can be named is not the eternal Tao."). To be seen, to have describable characteristics, energy must be excited, but the pure energy of which the Vacuum is composed is absolutely still, a sea of energy undisturbed by waves. It is when energy gets excited, when it becomes waves in the electromagnetic field, that we can see it, or when it condenses into particles of matter that we can touch and weigh it. As the quantum physicist David Bohm expressed it,

> In QFT, there is no such thing as empty space. "What we call empty space contains an immediate background of energy. Matter, as we know it, is a small, 'quantized' wave-like excitation on the top of the background [field], rather like a tiny ripple on a vast sea."[1]

The Quantum Vacuum is the ultimate, background energy field upon which what we take to be reality is "waving." Potentiality is the invisible, pregnant source of all actuality, the unseen face of the seen. And yet, though unseen, it is this residual potentiality, the pregnant Absence, within the Presence we do see, that gives the actual world its direction, animating force, and meaning. As the 17th-century Ming Dynasty philosopher Wang Fuzhi wrote about what is not directly expressed in Chinese poetry, "The breath animating the ink reaches the infinite in every direction, and even in the blank spaces of the text the meaning is omnipresent." Chinese poetry is sparse in its expression, leaving much unsaid for the reader to imagine for himself. In traditional Chinese paintings, the Absence, represented by mist, clouds, lakes, and the sky itself, draws our attention to unseen features and qualities of landscape figures that are Present.

In *The Art of War*, Sun Tzu advises military leaders to look for what is *not* evident in the field of battle, to look for the hidden tendencies latent within the situation and to adapt their strategies accordingly. Chapter 11 of the *Tao te Ching* says, "The wheel has thirty spokes, but it is the hole at the centre that holds it together. The vase is made of clay, but it is the emptiness inside that makes it useful." [The Chinese language itself expresses no gender, verbs have no temporal framework denoting past, present, or future, adjectives can be verbs, and nouns can be verbs or adjectives – all is left for the listener's interpretation. And what is *not* said in a conversation is often considered more important than what *is* said.] "Consequently," the *I Ching* advises, "the superior man treats with extreme care even that not visible to him; and treats with apprehension even that beyond the reach of his hearing.... Nothing is more manifest than the hidden, nothing more obvious than the subtle."[2]

A quantum business leader, too, will look for, and have strategies ready for, those hidden potentialities upon which the future and success of his company depends: the potential for geopolitical or environmental disruption, the potential for future pandemics like COVID, the unseen potential in matter to become objects or technologies of use, unseen potential in employee inventiveness, unseen potential in customer needs, unseen potential in the market situation, etc. This is the Nothingness from which the company's Being emerges. It is always present and always has consequences for both sustainability and innovation. A leader increases access to his company's potential by fostering a questioning, experimenting environment, and encouraging employees to question how things work, to wonder how things could be different, or improved, to experiment with new methods or products, and to question customers on what new things or changes they might like. Each question or experiment is like dropping a bucket into the sea of potentiality and bringing up a bucketful of new actuality.

- *A Universe Made of Energy*

We have seen that the Quantum Vacuum, the source and ground state of everything that exists, is a field of pure energy, and the ancient Chinese said the same thing about the originating Great Absence. In the 11th century A.D., the early Neo-Confucian philosopher Zhang Zai wrote that energy, *ch'i,* is the origin of all things, and that all existing things are in fact formations of energy, that the world as we know it, and we ourselves, are made of energy. Zhang Zai described matter as "concretised energy," as patterns or movements of energy that are oscillating at differing intensities. Following, and getting in tune with, these cosmic and natural rhythms through bodily movement is the rationale of the martial art *Tai Ch'i.* The purpose of Chinese acupuncture is to clear any blocks in the flow of *ch'i* throughout the body. A thousand years later, the equations and experiments of quantum field theory proved Zhang Zai's intuition to be a scientific reality.

"Taking this into account," asked the great quantum physicist Wolfgang Pauli, "what remains of the old ideas of matter and substance? The answer is *energy*. This is the true substance [of which everything is made], that which is conserved; only the form in which it occurs is changing." And accurately echoing the earlier words of Zhang Zai, physicist David Bohm stated, "What we call matter is actually condensed or frozen light." Photons, the "particles" of light, are massless bundles of pure energy. The word "quantum" itself refers to the smallest unit of energy required to make anything move or happen.

Everything that we can see, touch, and measure in our human world is a pattern of dynamic energy. Our own bodies are patterns of energy. We are energy, body, mind, and spirit. And the human organisations that we build are further patterns of dynamic energy. A quantum business leader will realise this and think about the daily processes and relationships in his company in a different way, now seeing the company as an energy system. He will see plant, skills, employees, and their labour as the company's stock of energy. He will see relationships between his company and the surrounding environment, relationships between company sectors and employees, relationships between employees and customers as patterns of energy flow, and in wanting to make the company more efficient, he will look for blocks or interruptions in these flows of energy.

Keeping the energy up, keeping the energy flowing, will be a key task of leadership. The quantum leader will see employee motivation and commitment as levels of energy and be sensitive to the overall energy level and dynamics of the company. Negative employee motivations like boredom (from too much routine, too little autonomy or too little responsibility) or fear (of making mistakes, of being scolded) suck energy out of the company system; positive motivations like team spirit, a sense of empowerment, creativity, or service pump energy into the system. A strong sense of company purpose is a powerful motivator, and thus the powerful source of energy.

- *A Changing, Uncertain, Non-determinate Universe*

  The dragon is the classic symbol of China. Chinese dragons are always portrayed as having perpetually moving, indefinite forms, like clouds on a windy afternoon. The dragon's constantly undulating body is ceaselessly and unpredictably evolving, now taking on this shape, then another. Filled with energy and potentiality, the dragon reminds us that all is change. In a similar way, landscape features in Chinese paintings are always depicted with diffuse, slightly out-of-focus lines, and the mountains, clouds, and waterfalls portrayed seem to be in constant movement. The *I Ching*, or *Book of Changes*, the foundational classic of Chinese thought, opens with the words, "The Way of Heaven ('the initiating,' 'the creative') is change and transformation," and the book itself is a guide to responding wisely to changing circumstances. China's greatest thinkers stress the uncertainty of this constant, dynamic change, and counsel remaining ever spontaneous when making decisions or plans. "The sage does a thing when the time comes," wrote Wang Yangming. "The study of changing conditions and events is to be done at the time of response." Even in modern China, plans and schedules are never fixed, decisions never finalised, until the last possible moment. All this is very quantum. And often very unsettling for Western visitors who prefer predictability and well-planned schedules!

Unlike Newtonian physics, which described an orderly, predictable, determinate world, quantum physics rests on the Uncertainty Principle. Quantum transformations happen constantly and spontaneously, and wholly unpredictably. The quantum world is "messy" and indeterminate, and in knowing what next to expect of a quantum system, scientists can rely only on probabilities. In quantum physics, even the laws of physics themselves have a dragon-like mutability, responding spontaneously to the surrounding environment, with bits of constituent stuff emerging now as particles, now as waves, sometimes "now," other times "then."

The environment in which 21st-century business operates is similarly messy and unpredictable and distinguished by constant, rapid change. Events like the COVID pandemic or the wars in Ukraine and Gaza spring up overnight, new materials and new technologies appear on an almost weekly basis, consumer tastes are fickle, and the choices available are multiple. Markets and events are interlinked and complex, and complexity is unpredictable. A quantum leader would follow Wang Yangming's advice and respond appropriately only at the moment of necessary decision. A company's five-year plan may be a guiding vision, but daily strategy must be constantly adaptive, company structures designed to be agile and responsive, company identity itself perhaps diverse and fluid, experimentation constant, greater risk embraced but spread.

- *A Universe Made of Relationships*

Chinese thought has always stressed the interconnectedness of everything. The *Tao te Ching* tells us that everything is connected to everything, everything inside everything, I am in the world, and the world is within me. Both Daoism and Confucianism stress the critical importance of relationships and see the individual as someone defined by his network of relationships. In arguing that the universe is made of *ch'i*, Zhang Zai says the transformation of the Great Absence into the 10,000 Present things is relational, that *ch'i* coalesces into matter through the forming of relationships: "It is the function of nature to combine." Zhu Xi, whose own interpretation of the Tao is that it is the One Principle from which all things originate, tells us that the *Tao* expresses itself as "one principle with many manifestations." That same one principle defines and relates the nature of Chinese military strategy, ideas of governance, art, poetry, and medicine. And still in modern China, people devote great effort to building their relationships, trusting them more than contracts. Every Chinese person has his *guanxi* – his circle of special relationships.

The universe described in Newton's physics is a reality composed of separate, isolated, atomistic particles – things, objects. It is a fragmented, static reality. But quantum science has caught up with what the Chinese always knew. In contrast to Newton's view, the quantum universe is entangled and coherent. Everything "hangs together," everything progresses as a unified whole – a flowing, ever-changing whole. Everything is connected to everything, everything is inside of everything, everything *is* everything. Indeed, quantum field theory tells us that the universe is *made* of relationships. In my book, *The Quantum Self,* I wrote,

> For the quantum self, a relationship is not a relationship between 'I' and 'you' or between 'I' and 'it' in which you or it (anything in your surrounding physical environment) influences *me*. For the quantum self, I and you seem to influence *each other*, we seem to 'get inside' each other and to change each other, simultaneously, from *within* in such a way that 'I' and 'you' become '*we*'. This 'we' that we experience is not just 'I' *and* 'you', it is a new thing in itself, a new unity. The 'we' that we become takes on its own, new identity, with its own capacity for further relationships.[3]

This is an example of quantum emergence – something becoming larger than the sum of its parts.

In quantum physics, relationship replaces the usual understanding of causality. Events happen, or situations develop, because of changing patterns of relationships. The same is true of our human world. We are a social, relational species, and our relationships define us. As David Bohm expresses it, "We are all connected and operate within living fields of thought and experience." Change our relationships, and we change ourselves. Change the relationships that have brought about an undesirable situation, and the situation will improve. If we want to make the world a better place, build better relationships.

Companies, too, are made of relationships and enjoy success or failure depending upon the existence and quality of these. Companies work more effectively and harmoniously when barriers between people, levels of authority, and functions are removed. That is why Quantum Management urges "no borders." Quantum companies thrive because they are ecosystems. Employees and multifunctional teams are connected to and cooperate with each other, employees know their customers and have built interactive, co-creative relationships with them, relationships are built with partnering companies, and even with competitors where beneficial, and these companies take seriously their relationship with the environment and the surrounding community.

- *Holism – The Universe is a System*

The holistic nature of the universe follows directly from the fact that, as both Chinese thought and quantum physics have seen, everything is related to everything. Both tell us there is no such thing as separation. To quote David Bohm, "Separation is an illusion." Nothing and no one is an island unto itself. Everything exists in a context of relationships, everything is a part of the larger whole that is our universe and the world of living things. A famous principle in physics, Mach's principle, states, "The whole is necessary to the understanding of its parts, as the parts are necessary to the understanding of the whole." To understand any situation, to deal effectively with any problem or challenge, we must consider the entire context of the relationships within which it is situated, consider everything that is acting upon it and everything that it is acting upon. This is what Sun Tzu meant when he advised military strategists to "know the field" and to "know the enemy." Such insight is the basis of systems thinking, and the Chinese have always been natural systems thinkers. Systems thinking is also an essential feature of Quantum Management.

As an example of systems thinking at work in a company's strategic thinking, consider the challenges facing a food ingredients supplier I have been working with recently. They want to significantly grow their market in Africa. Hoping to become a responsible quantum company, their strategic goal is two-fold: to offer products that are good, and sustainable for public health, and to increase their profit margins while doing so. Aware they are working in an African context, systems thinking tells company leaders they must consider certain market features and challenges specific to that region. I will mention four.

Africa has long been a dumping ground for unwholesome products rejected by Western consumers. In this context, offering healthy and sustainable food ingredients will give the company a competitive advantage over competing suppliers. In the developed world, annual meat consumption per capita is 18 kg per person, but in Africa, this averages only 6 kg. Africans need more protein, but increasing cattle production in Africa would be bad for the environment. Taking this context into account, the company strategy is to offer more, and better tasting, plant-based meat substitutes. Fizzy drink consumption is increasing in Africa, but most fizzy drinks on offer there are laden with sugar or cheap sugar substitutes now considered unhealthy in the West. Fizzy drinks also, traditionally, have no nutritional value. In response, the company's r&d people are developing natural sugar substitutes and nutritional additives like probiotics. Finally, meeting the demands of the fizzy drinks market is currently a large share of the company's portfolio. But fizzy drinks consume huge quantities of water, and Africa faces drought caused by climate change. Water will be scarce, expensive, and consuming large quantities unnecessarily, environmentally irresponsible. Looking ahead to this problem, the company is now making moves to be less dependent on this market. Each of these decisions has been made taking the broader context within which the company is active into account. Systems thinking and Quantum Management in action.

- *Dynamic Polarity – Process of All Transformation*

  A fundamental feature of both quantum physics and Chinese thought is not to focus on things, situations, or events in their static being, but rather to focus on the *process* of their movement as they change. Reality never stands still; nothing ever remains the same. As Confucius said, "Everything flows on and on like this river, without pause, day and night."[4] In the Chinese tradition, this is the purpose of consulting the *I Ching*: to understand the movement or direction of change in a situation and to learn the most effective way to work *with* that movement. And for the Chinese, all change and transformation is driven by the dynamic *yin/yang* polarity. This, perhaps more than anything else about Chinese thought, distinguishes it from traditional Western understanding and foreshadows that of quantum physics.

  In nearly all Western thought, polarities are thought of as being opposite and opposing. Black is the opposite of white, good the opposite of bad, beauty the opposite of ugliness, etc. This necessary either/or opposition or exclusion of opposites sits at the very heart of Western logic, monotheism, and today's zero-sum strategic thinking. But the Chinese *yin/yang* polarity is *complimentary*. The two support each other, the two work together as an overall transformational dynamic, and the two are *inside* each other. As Zhang Zai expressed it, "The essence of *yin* and *yang* is that each conceals within itself the dwelling place of the other."[5] Thus we read in the *Tao te Ching*:

  The whole world recognises the beautiful as the beautiful, only because there is the ugly;

  > The whole world recognizes the good as the good,
  > only because there is the bad;
  > Thus Something and Nothing produce each other;
  > The difficult and the easy complement each other;
  > The long and the short off-set each other;
  > The high and the low incline towards each other;
  > Note and sound harmonize with each other;
  > Before and after follow each other.[6]

  This mutually supportive, mutually dependent, and dynamic polarity is, of course, also the essence of wave/particle duality in today's quantum physics – the mysterious, "illogical" heart of quantum physics that Niels Bohr had to turn to the Chinese *I Ching* to make any sense of.

Quantum wave/particle duality is a co-creative dialogue between potentiality and actuality, between the unseen Absence, the not yet realised, and the seen Presence, the already realised, the transformation dynamic between creation, destruction, and re-creation. Before they are observed or measured, quantum entities exist as a wave-like array of superimposed potentialities spread out all over space and time. Once they are observed or measured, they manifest as particles with a fixed identity and location. The quirky effect of observation on quantum waves is illustrated by the famous Schrodinger's cat, who is *both* alive *and* dead while concealed in a closed box, but is found to be *either* alive *or* dead once the box is opened and he is observed. But as all cats have nine lives, even the dead quantum cat may live to see another day!

Just as *yin* is always present within *yang*, and *yang* is always present within *yin*, the many potentialities of a quantum wave are always present within the manifested particle, and the manifested particle is always exerting an influence on the accompanying wave. Absence and Presence are intertwined, stuff of the same substance. As the *Tao te Ching* says, "In perennial Absence you see mystery, and in perennial Presence you see appearance. Though the two are one and the same, once they arise, they differ in name." This *yin/yang*-like dynamic polarity of wave/particle duality is at the heart of every transformation, at every level of reality – in the cosmos, in the natural world, and in our human lives, projects, personalities, and thoughts, and in our company system dynamics.

Quantum companies, of course, have their *yin/yang* or wave/particle dynamic. This means that a company's future decisions, products, or services are already implied or suggested within the decisions made and the products or services being offered today, and, in turn, future decisions, products, or services will be influenced by the current situation. The transformation dynamic at play in this dialogue between a company's present and its future is mirrored in the company's complimentary capacities for creative destruction on the one hand and innovation on the other. Thus, the sustainability of a company depends upon its constant renewal through these processes. It is common sense to most business leaders that a failure to innovate limits the lifespan of their company. A critical argument I make for the benefits of Quantum Management, which emphasises this *yin/yang* dynamic, is that it can greatly increase innovation potential, and thus company lifespan – indeed even has the possibility to confer on a company the near immortality of a living ecosystem like a great city, a tropical rainforest, or Gaia itself.

The quantum universe is in constant, *indeterminate* flux, a process of contingent and uncertain change. Both *yin/yang* and quantum wave/particle duality thrive on this indeterminism and the diverse possibilities of the unfolding future. For a quantum company, the future is always open, and therefore, it must always be ready to meet it. That is why agility and the capacity for spontaneous adaptation are critical. The organisational principles advocated by Quantum Management, calling for the elimination of cumbersome bureaucracy and siloed work functions, and greater front-line employee decision making, assure this.

Notes

1 David Bohm, *Wholeness and the Implicate Order*.
2 *Doctrine of the Mean*, 1:2 and 1:3.
3 Danah Zohar, *The Quantum Self*, 110.
4 *Analects*, ix, 16.
5 Zhang Zai, *Zengmeng*, 12.
6 David Hinton, *Tao te Ching*, Chapter 2.

2 Companies as Part of the Living World

The Tang dynasty poem Tao Yuanming, *A Ballad of Peach Blossom Spring*, mirrors the powerful role that nature, and seeing human life as intimately a part of nature, has played in Chinese life, art, and thought:

> The fisherman paddled up the stream. He loved spring in the mountains;
> peach blossoms along the bank clustered by the ancient ford.
> He passed through a narrow gap in the mountains, a dark and twisted way.
> Then the mountain opened out onto a broad flat plain.
> Far off, he glimpsed something among the clouds and trees.
> Coming closer, he saw a thousand homes amid flowers and bamboo.
> Dwelling together here by their magical spring,
> They created a world of their own.
> At night, the moon shone down through pines on their quiet homes;
> When the sun rose through the clouds, chickens crowed and dogs barked.

As he paddles along, the fisherman's awareness and sense of place encompass not just the stream but all the surrounding mountains, vegetation and animal life, the clouds and the moon, and the "thousand homes" dwelling amidst all. Each is a part of each, and each a part of a greater all, and they "create a world of their own."

The *shanshui*, mountain and water tradition in Chinese painting illustrates this same intimate connection. Human dwellings and human figures are always portrayed nestling securely in mountain settings, trees and either lakes or streams nearby. The *I Ching* tells us that human beings can only produce the right thoughts, and thus have the right actions, if we conform to the laws of nature: "The fulfilment of Nature, which is Life in perpetual creativity, is the gate of Wisdom bringing forth the value of Tao and the principle of righteousness." Nature is the essence of the Good and the source of righteousness, and hence the way to construct and govern our lives. It is our Home.

DOI: 10.4324/9781003623267-4

How very different this is from Western ideas about the relationship between nature and our human lives! The traditional Western view has been that we humans are different from, apart from, and above the natural order. The creations of the natural world are there for our use and exploitation, nature itself a wild and dangerous force we must fear and try to control. Consider this passage from Goethe's *Sorrows of Young Werther*:

> Nature has formed nothing that does not consume itself, and every object near it: so that, surrounded by earth and air and all active powers, I wander on my way with an aching heart; the universe is to me a fearful monster, forever devouring its own offspring.

For the Chinese, Heaven, Earth, Man, and our human social endeavours are all part of one harmonious and balanced system. We have seen that in Chinese culture, military strategy, good governance, medicine, and art all follow the same set of principles that are outlined in Chinese philosophy and that these principles reflect the way of Heaven (the way of the cosmos and nature). Confucius said,

> The moral laws form one system with the laws by which Heaven and Earth support and contain, overshadow and canopy all things. These moral laws form the same system with the laws by which the seasons succeed each other and the sun and the moon appear with the alterations of day and night.... It is this, one system running through all, that makes the universe so impressively great.[1]

One thousand years later, quantum science has established this as a scientific fact.

In scientists' descriptions of our quantum universe at its many levels of order and reality, we see the same laws and principles being expressed in originating cosmic events, in the evolutionary processes of life here on Earth, within the cells of our own bodies, and in the ways that our spontaneous social activities organise and unfold. When we look at how our consciousness and minds work in Chapter 4, we will see these same principles at work in many of the ways we think and know our world. Further, "The all-encompassing order of Nature extends to the sociopolitical level," wrote the neo-Taoist philosopher Wang Bi, "the institution of the family and that of the state are not extrinsic to Nature." Nearly 3000 years later, leading complexity scientist Geoffrey West might have continued Wang Bi's thought by adding, "And neither is the company!"

In 2017, West, Director of America's pioneering Santa Fe Institute, published his book *Stages*, with the subtitle, "The Universal Laws of Life and Death in Organisms, Cities, and Companies." This book added further scientific credibility to ancient Chinese intuition. Complexity science originally crossed the divide between physics and living science with its discovery of Complex Adaptive Systems – quantum physics expressing itself through living systems. Each of the defining principles of quantum physics for non-living systems has its match in the principles of complexity science that apply to living systems. Complex adaptive systems (CADs) are systems in which all constituent parts simultaneously both *affect* each other and are *affected by* each other. Further, this internal, mutual adaptation between its own parts is accompanied by a simultaneous, mutual adaptation between the organism and its external environment. The whole ensemble, system plus environment, is one dynamic, interactive, and co-creative "super system" in which a complex array of non-linear feedback loops defy the laws of cause and effect. James Lovelock's Gaia hypothesis, which proposes a mutual and self-regulating relationship between the Earth's living organisms and their non-living environment, describes such a complex adaptive dynamic.

In fact, all living systems, from the most simple bacteria to our human selves, are CADs, and these thrive, sustain themselves, and creatively evolve employing the same principles of spontaneity (indeterminism), holism, contextuality, and self-organisation that underpin the working of our quantum universe. CADs are, in principle, living quantum systems. Then, as though making quantum physics come alive were not enough, the insights of complexity science were extended to make companies come alive. West and his Santa Fe Institute colleague, Nobel Prize economist Brian Arthur,[2] demonstrated that human organisational systems like the global economy, spontaneous social groups, and cities are also best understood as CADs, and our companies, if allowed to self-organise, will best thrive and continue to grow when these same organising principles are at play. Companies, too, have the capacity to be living systems. Complexity science, like traditional Chinese thought, is telling us that, as things *are* in nature, so they *should,* or would *best, be* in our human order.

Today's more aware company leaders are seeking new ideas for better structuring and managing their organisations. They realise that companies organised and led in the usual way, with strong top-down management control and an inflexible, pyramidal power structure mediated by a great deal of bureaucracy are struggling, and often failing, in a new business reality defined by uncertainty, rapid change, and an undeniable connectivity with supposed externalities like the success or failure of competitors, climate and economic instability, global political rivalries, health pandemics, and socio-economic conditions in their own or "distant" regions and countries. All of these factors affect supply chains as well as customer choice and demand. Nothing in our universe exists in isolation, and companies can no longer presume they are islands unto themselves.

Based on the discoveries of complexity science, Quantum Management tells us that companies can best ensure sustainability, constant innovation, and growth when they fully take their place alongside every other living thing and become part of nature – to become CADs themselves. Company leaders must realise they are *not* engineers skilfully operating machines, but rather stewards of nature looking over and nourishing their organisations as a good farmer would tend to and nourish his growing crops.

How Do Quantum Companies Function as CADs?

In bold outline, for companies to become CADs, Quantum Management calls for an end to strong top-down control, removal of bureaucracy and the pyramidal power structure, and replacing these with distributed decision-making by an interconnected network of small, self-organising, and multifunctional teams that each maintains a close, interactive relationship with customers, other companies, and society. To better understand why these are natural features of a company operating as a CAD, let us look more closely at how they mirror the defining qualities of such a system.

- *Self-Organising:* Complex adaptive systems are self-organising systems. This means they are driven from *inside*, by an internal logic of their own. No outside agent has designed them, and no outside or central force controls them. It is as though they have a kind of self-aware consciousness, or inner compass, that just "knows" how best to grow and adapt as needed. Indeed, complexity science has discovered that *if* any kind of outside interference or control *is* applied to such a system, it immediately disrupts the system's self-organising capacity and the system loses its vitality and evolutionary capacity. It dies. Such spontaneous self-organisation is unknown to the mainstream of Western thought.

  While the Chinese have always believed that the *Tao*, the organising principle in the universe, unfolds spontaneously and unpredictably, Western thought has always believed in a universe that was *designed,* either by God or by Reason. Even Newton believed that God had designed the laws of physics, which then, in turn, rigidly control all events, just as a blueprint design and an overriding control system govern a machine. Newton, we have seen, compared the universe to a giant, clockwork machine. This is why Western management, inspired by Newtonian physics, believes that companies should be designed and controlled to operate as reliable, predictable machines. But companies are now having to cope in a digital, quantum age. Quantum technologies have created a world that is fast, interconnected, and more self-organising. The new AI technologies that are appearing on factory floors are at first programmed, with algorithms designed into them, but they then "think" with a self-organising capacity of their own, and produce surprising results that feel out of our human control. This is why we are finding AI an increasingly frightening spectacle. We feel we may be controlled *by* it.

  Quantum companies, inspired by the more indeterminate and organic worldview arising from quantum physics and complexity science, and viewed as living systems rather than machines, are self-organising companies. They, too, must be free of destructive top-down control, and that means free of Western-style top-down leadership. The dynamic company system must be trusted to "know what it is doing," the company's more front-line employees trusted to know what is best, and thus to have autonomy and decision-making power. The former Managing Director of Britain's Marks & Spencer, Andrew Stone, once wrote to me, "I work for a company that seems to have a brain of its own, and even when we all go home at night, this brain continues to think." Zhang Ruimin, the recently retired CEO of Haier, who conceived the *RenDanHeYi* management model, said that as a young man, it was his ambition to run a company where its employees were allowed to think. Following the implementation in 2012 of *RenDanHeYi,* Zhang's surrender of top-down leadership, and the reorganisation of Haier into 4000 autonomous, multifunctional, customer-facing "microenterprises," Haier employees working on those small teams were empowered to make all decisions concerning their team activities, to hire any new team members desired, and to decide for themselves how to allocate profits made by each team. Each microenterprise became an independent company in its own right, and the umbrella company motto became, "At Haier, everyone is a leader." This motto might equally have been, "At Haier, everyone is a thinker."

- *The Edge of Chaos:* Faced with uncertainty and unpredictable change, most leaders who follow the traditional, "business-as-usual" paradigm are tempted to slam on the brakes, tighten up control. Indeed, the standard wisdom of "business-as-usual" is to nurture stability, reduce uncertainty wherever possible, minimise disturbances, and "manage risk." Those traditional leaders who do look to nature for lessons in management commonly cite our body's immune system as an example, describing how the immune system "stabilises itself" to ward off infection. But this is precisely what the immune system does *not* do! The invading viruses and bacteria that make us ill are constantly mutating, always trying to outsmart the body's immune defences. They are, after all, adaptive systems themselves. The only way the immune system can stay one step ahead of the invaders is to be poised at the edge of *instability,* to be ready to spontaneously evolve in any direction required, at a moment's notice.

  It is instability that underpins the immune system's own flexibility, its adaptability. In scientific terms, this zone of radical instability is known as "the edge of chaos," the creative meeting point between order and chaos. And indeed, many of our human biological functions, such as our sense of smell and the way our brains process vision, are poised at the edge of chaos, as are innovative thought and most of our learning ability. A human infant's brain is poised at the edge of chaos. The near-chaotic instability in the way its neurones fire enables the infant to rapidly adapt to the physical and cultural conditions in which it has been born. It is precisely this internal chaos, this "messiness" that enables our brains to be nature's most effective "learning organisations" and children its most promising pupils. Among creative adults – artists, musicians, poets, brilliant scientists – a far higher than average percentage "suffer" some degree of mental instability.

The "edge of chaos" is critical to understanding why messiness and instability are important ingredients of company innovation. The concept was first introduced into science by Ilya Prigogine, a Nobel Prize-winning pioneer in the foundations of complexity science. Prigogine distinguished between "closed systems" and "open systems."[3] Closed systems operate entirely within their own boundaries and have a one-way relationship with their surroundings. They may, like any machine, generate energy or motion and create an effect in the surrounding environment, but they are not themselves internally changed by anything from outside. They are stable and predictable, but not at all creative – islands unto themselves. "Open systems," by contrast, are in a constant, co-creative dialogue with their environment, themselves undergoing changes within as they interact with, and have an effect on, the environment in which they find themselves. They have no hard and fast boundaries, no fixed, determinate structure, are unstable and unpredictable – but ever creative. Open systems create order out of chaos, they feed on "mess." All CADs – all living systems – are open systems. Quantum companies that closely interact with their customers and their changing needs and tastes, reinventing themselves accordingly, are open systems. They must have flexible (unstable!) infrastructures, strategies, and modes of operation that are poised at the edge of chaos. And though poised at the edge, open systems have the capacity to *create new order* that is both stable and dynamic. Innovative companies create new working practices and new products and services.

It is the wrong-headed belief that stability and predictability are good for business that has made bureaucracy so attractive to companies. Bureaucracy slows things down, eliminates "rash decisions," and ensures commands from the top are carried out. It does this by organising all the disparate departments, functions, and employees in a company into a rigidly connected, pyramidal power structure through which a chain of commands can filter slowly, being checked by a middle manager at every stage. Bureaucracy's main theorist, Max Weber, described it as "an iron cage." But, as proven by an important theorem in cybernetics – Von Foerster's Theorem –

The more rigidly connected are the elements of a system, the less influence they will have on the system as a whole.... The more rigid the connections, the more each element of the system will exhibit a greater degree of 'alienation' from the whole.[4]

In short, bureaucracy destroys the vitality and holism of natural organisms. Its rigid structures impose clear boundaries, and break organisations up into separate, siloed parts and functions, none of which has any effective grasp of the overall company purpose or strategy. Employees working in siloed functions and simply following rules and commands have little grasp of their own purpose or the final outcome of their day's labour. They have no agency or power. Hence, the "alienation." Bureaucracy turns a living system like a company into a mere machine, predictable, stable, and controllable, but of narrow use and limited life span. And it turns human employees into mere mechanical parts. This is why Quantum Management calls for eliminating it, instead encouraging company leaders to follow the advice of someone like the great theatre director Peter Brook.

Known for his advocacy of last-minute improvisation, Brook explained his dislike of fixed stage sets designed in advance by famous sculptors or artists, saying that, imposed from the outside, they can constrain and take the life out of a production. "What is necessary," he said,

> is an incomplete design; a design that has clarity without rigidity; one that can be called 'open' as against 'shut'.... A true theatre designer will think of his designs being all the time in motion, in action, in relation to what the actor brings to the scene as it unfolds. The later he makes his decisions, the better.[5]

Chinese paintings, living organisms, and quantum companies *move*; they have life. Our bodies, our minds, and our companies don't just tolerate uncertainty. They *use* it and *thrive* because of it. They have those qualities we find so delightful in a child. They are exploratory, creative, "playful," like nature itself.

- *Flexible/Adaptive:* Today's uncertainty and rapid change challenge companies constantly to adapt. CADs can be so adaptive because their internal structure is flexible. Like our human brains, their structures are "plastic," easily changed. Nothing is "fixed in place," nothing "locked down," so they are free to adapt quickly when confronted with new challenges or opportunities. Both Chinese thought and quantum science celebrate the uncertainty of changes and events. The entirety of the *I Ching* is devoted to helping its readers deal wisely with this uncertainty, and Daoism, Ch'an Buddhism, and Confucianism all stress the importance of spontaneity for responding quickly to the uncertainty of events. Both Chinese art and calligraphy demand the spontaneous, emotional expression of the artist or brush holder. Quantum physics, of course, stresses that all changes are "indeterminate," and itself rests upon the Uncertainty Principle. Quantum Management calls upon companies to be flexible and spontaneous, always poised to change plans or decisions in quick response to the rapid change and uncertainty within the business environment.

The importance of this flexible spontaneity in today's world is, of course, one key reason for ridding quantum companies of cumbersome bureaucracy and distributing power to a network of smaller, autonomous teams. Employees must be able to make decisions quickly, without waiting for clearance from a long chain of bureaucratic overlords. Another reason for clearing out the bureaucracy is, as noted above, the creative potential of uncertainty itself. Uncertainty usually accompanies the mess and chaos that precede creativity. Uncertainty is not just desirable, it is *necessary*.

To ensure their own adaptability, the small, self-organising teams of quantum companies have a flexible make-up. Their defining boundaries are porous. Team members may come and go as their skills are best suited, first to one team then perhaps to another. The teams, like the company itself, are constantly reinventing themselves. During their own quantum organisational transformation, the very chairs and desks of Volvo engineers were equipped with wheels so they could move easily between different teams during the working day.

- *Holistic:* Like all quantum systems, CADs are holistic – everything is related to everything, and everything is responsive to everything. As Chinese medicine has always understood, every organ in the body of a living system is connected with and responsive to every other organ, and all organs are responsive to any changes in the system as a whole. The body cannot be broken down into a collection of separate organs, and any disease or malfunction must be seen as a weakness of the whole system and treated as such. Indeed, no quantum system can be understood by breaking it down into smaller parts. No part makes any sense except in its relation to the whole, and that whole is always greater than the sum of its parts.

Quantum companies do everything possible to eliminate boundaries, barriers and borders, both internally and externally. Thus, while a company using its own adaptation of the Haier *RenDanHeyi* model may have been transformed into a collection of small, independent teams, these teams are connected in a dynamic network in which all communicate with and cooperate with all. The company is an emergent reality larger than the sum of its parts. And all small teams are in a close, interactive and co-creative relationship with customers. The employees of a quantum company *know* their customers. Relying not just upon digital customer satisfaction surveys, team members actually speak with customers, sometimes visit their homes. Sales personnel remember birthdays, attend weddings and funerals. The sales force at Roche India approached doctors and hospital directors with "How can I help you?," not "What can I sell you?"

A quantum company's network of teams and customers, taken together, functions as a living ecosystem like *Gaia itself,* each part constantly adapting to changes in other parts and to changes in the surrounding environment. Changing customer needs and tastes become ideas for new products and new service arrangements, and these, in turn, bring a better quality of life to customers. Customers of Haier are invited to submit new products or technological ideas and are rewarded for doing so. Some quantum companies, like Haier, include other companies, sometimes even competitors, within their ecosystem to offer joint, scenario products or joint ventures.

Quantum companies also build strong relationships with their local communities. They contribute funds to local projects, provide training opportunities to local people, perhaps allow their facilities to be used by members of the community, and pay their taxes. GE Electronics in America allows local students to use their First Build design and engineering laboratory after school. The Dahan Group in China provided funds to build a large traditional crafts training centre for local school students. A glass company in Slovenia allowed local residents to use its sports centre. In Part III of this book, we will see more detailed examples of how several Chinese companies thrive because of this more holistic relationship with customers and the community.

- *Purposive.* Both traditional Chinese thought and quantum science also stress that both the universe and nature are driven by a sense of elemental purpose – that there are organisational principles at play that drive them in a recognisable direction. Remember that quantum physics tells us the universe has a drive towards relationships and that all reality is *made* of relationships. This cosmic drive towards ever more relationships is a drive towards the creation of ever more complexity and thus ever more information. It can be said that this expansion of complexity and information is the universe's driving purpose. CADs are exploratory and evolutionary, always driven towards growth. Sustainability and growth are their purpose. More advanced living organisms also contain more genetic information. And information contains meaning. Thus, a quantum physicist like David Bohm argues that the universe itself, including nature, is filled with meaning or, indeed, even made of meaning.

Our human lives, too, are driven by a need for, and a search for, purpose and meaning. In my own work on SQ, spiritual intelligence, I pointed out that we will sacrifice a great deal, sometimes life itself, for an activity or a cause that has meaning to us. This search for meaning, a sense that our lives or activities are meaningful, that they *matter*, that they make a *difference*, is the basis of all our positive motivations. Traditional management practice that sees employees simply as instruments of production and expects them just to follow orders "from above" and do as they are told, overlooks this. That is why so many companies today are failing to benefit from the fact that most workers are now better educated and have expectations that go beyond simply earning a salary. Increasing numbers of, particularly younger employees, are now demanding intangibles like a sense of purpose and meaning in their work, and a greater opportunity to realise their potential. They want to act, to make decisions, and to feel their work is making a difference. When they are denied these things, motivation and thus energy drop, their health suffers, absenteeism and attrition rates rise, and productivity remains low.

Because Quantum Management is dealing with human systems, an important part of the theory argues that the purposes, values, aspirations, and motivations of employees working in an organisation, and the emergent organisational culture, must be considered as part of any successful company's system dynamics. Thus, the leader of a quantum company always provides clear direction by asking, "What is our purpose? What are our values? What motivations must drive our people?" Understanding this very well, when Lara Bezerra was Managing Director of Roche India, she changed her job title to Chief Purpose Officer. She inspired her employees by giving their jobs a sense of higher purpose, telling them they were not mere salesmen, but rather, doctors' helpers, themselves playing an important role in bringing better health care to the people of India. And just as employees will often take a cut in salary to take a job that offers them more sense of meaning and purpose, a company's purpose cannot be limited to the mere pursuit of profit. The broader purpose must be something meaningful, something that inspires and motivates people to want to give the best of themselves, and that inspires and motivates customer loyalty. A purpose-driven company fits well into our purpose-driven universe.

Notes

1 Taken from *The Doctrine of the Mean*.
2 W. Brian Arthur, *Complexity and the Economy*.
3 Ilya Prigogine and Isabelle Stengers, *Order Out of Chaos*.
4 Benny Shannon and Henri Atlan, "Von Foerster's Theorem on Connectedness and Organization," 81–90.
5 Peter Brook, *The Empty Space*, 114.

3 The Higher Meaning of Leadership & Companies

To men and women leading companies, it may seem very strange to be told that their leadership practice plays a key role in the evolution of the universe. Yet Mencius reminds us that, "The 10,000 things are all brought to fruition by us." Understanding this is part of the mindset required to realise the meaning and significance of new paradigm Quantum Management. Seeing that all human beings, and particularly leaders, have a co-creative relationship with cosmic reality itself adds a larger dimension and meaning to our lives and leadership. It helps us to understand that leadership is a spiritual vocation, that it has a higher meaning and purpose, and a much greater responsibility, than simply ensuring that our companies are making a profit, and that the way we treat our employees is about much more than just assuring that they do what they are told. Quantum leaders are reality builders. They literally make the world, and all "the 10,000 things" their leadership brings to completion. And in doing so, yes, they are partners in cosmic evolution itself.

The vision I have just offered of the leader's truly significant relationship with the cosmos would not seem at all strange to someone familiar with China's traditional wisdom, of course. We have already seen that the Chinese have always believed that the Way of Heaven is the Way of Man. Chuang Tzu taught, "Heaven, Earth, and I are living together, and all things and I form an inseparable unity." Zhang Zai wrote, "I form the substance of all things without overlooking any, and all things form my substance," and "We are not mere creatures, but creators, and as such we have the power and responsibility to create and sustain the life and vitality of this world and ourselves...." And most fundamentally, because it is the origin of all Chinese thought, the *I Ching* describes human beings as "the bridge between Heaven and Earth," the bridge that carries all the potentiality and order latent within the larger cosmos (within the quantum vacuum) to the things we can build here on Earth – to the societies we build, to the way we live our human lives and the relationships we form, and to our companies.

All human beings serve as those bridges, but our leaders are the bridges that carry the most weight. They show others the way. Company leaders are the bridges that carry the raw materials of Heaven (the cosmos and nature) and turn them into the products and services that shape and enable our lives here on Earth. Every time a company innovates, it literally brings a new reality into being. In doing so, China's ancient sages said, they add to and enrich Heaven itself. The modern Chinese philosopher Thome Fang (Fang Dongmei) describes a co-creative "sympathetic unity" between man and the universe in which

> the creative advance of Man and the Universe proceed on the same track: 'I am the substance in the fullness of the universe; I am the leading vital impetus in the vast array of cosmic forces.... Man is never set apart from the universe and the universe is never set apart from man.'[1]

All such talk of co-creativity or sympathetic harmony between we humans, nature, and the cosmos has, of course, been alien to the mainstream of Western thought. Western people have always seen nature as hostile, something to be controlled or exploited. The Judeo/Christian Bible gives man "dominion over the earth." The universe seems vast and remote. And when a scientific understanding of the universe emerged in the 16th and 17th centuries, Newtonian physics assigned humans no part in it. We are just "observers," bystanders, and passive witnesses to a lifeless universe governed by mechanical laws. A prevailing Western sense of alienation, helplessness, and victimhood follows from this "we are strangers in a strange land" mindset. And now, in an age of space travel, we set out to "conquer" the universe, as we have been conquering nature. An "us against them," zero-sum mentality prevails between us and the universe. But were Western people better to understand the quantum science that they themselves discovered, a less defeatist and combative mindset could emerge.

A Participative Universe

Western logic has always made a sharp distinction between subjects and objects, between observers and what they observe. As an observer, I stand back from things and events, separate myself from them, and see them as "other," as objects or events that influence me or that I can act upon via some mode of external force. But quantum physics demonstrated that no such distinction can be made, no such separation exists. It describes a "participatory universe" in which the observer of any event, situation, or thing and the event, situation, or thing observed are co-creative partners in one dynamic process, akin to the Chinese *yin/yang* dynamic. The *way* I observe something, or interact with it, determines *what* I will observe. If my observation or interaction is different, what I observe or interact with will itself be different. And this is not just a difference of perspective. My observation or interaction actually determines the being, the reality, the actual physical properties or characteristics of what I observe. This creative nature of observation was powerfully demonstrated in quantum physics by the famous two-slit experiment.

As we saw earlier, early 20th-century physicists were puzzled by the question of whether light consists of a series of waves or of a stream of particles. They found that when they passed a beam of light (a beam of photons) through an opaque barrier in which either one or two slits could be left open, the number of open slits determined the nature of what they observed after the light beam had gone through the barrier. If the physicists opened just one slit in the barrier, the light emerged as a stream of particles that registered as a series of distinctive clicks in a photomultiplier tube. But if they opened both slits that the light could pass through, it emerged as a series of waves that created an interference pattern on a screen. As we discussed before, we now know that at the quantum level, light is *both* wave-like *and* particle-like. It is a superposition of the two potentialities. But what the two-slit experiment demonstrated so clearly was that, at our everyday level of reality, which side of its dual nature manifests as an actual, measurable entity depends upon how we choose to observe it. It is *we*, our acts of setting up the conditions of the observation, that create the entities we see.

We humans are not just *in* the world, not just observers *of* the world, we *make* the world. And in making our world, we create further potentialities that both transform that world and shape the universe itself. In making the present, we create the future. "We are the bees of the invisible," wrote the German poet Rainer Marie Rilke. "We madly gather the honey of the visible to store it in the great golden hive of the invisible."[2] In the language of quantum physics, we could say that we are "agents" of the quantum vacuum, transforming elements of the vast sea of potentiality stored within it into new actuality. Each one of us, every moment of every day, with the decisions and choices that we make and the actions that we take, is creating new realities, making the world, shaping the future. This is the true significance of business innovation, the true reason for nurturing the potential of every employee. There are no unimportant people, no lives without consequence, and no human beings who do not carry the infinite potential of the quantum vacuum within them. It is essential to the definition of our humanity that we are world creators. But how much greater the consequences of the decisions and choices made by leaders, and the actions they take. The companies they build become active agents of co-creation, almost living persons with brains that themselves then transform both "Heaven" and Earth.

Companies Are Conscious Agents, Too

The idea that individual companies have "brains" that function like conscious agents, much like those of human beings, was first suggested to me by Britain's Lord Andrew Stone in a letter he wrote introducing himself. Stone was then the Joint Global Managing Director of the retailing giant Marks & Spencer. Stone is one of a small number of Western business leaders who recognise openly that their leadership style has been strongly influenced by the images and ideas they have encountered from quantum science and the other new sciences of the 20th century that have followed its paradigm. "My work," he wrote,

> is in building that houses three thousand people who are essentially individual 'neurons' of the 'brain' of an organization that consists of sixty thousand people worldwide. The organization is seen to have its own identity (it has been in existence for over a hundred years), it has a mind and a will and an intelligence that exist in the absence of these people even when the offices are shut but is dependent on the interaction of the individuals from which it is constituted.

In later conversations with me, Lord Stone spoke of his company's ongoing personality and its instinct over the years for choosing leaders with different styles or visions because they were the leaders needed at that moment. "The company itself somehow functions above and beyond the actions and decisions of its individual members – the CEOs, the board chairmen, the employees, the shareholders, etc." Companies, too, like all other living systems, are self-organising systems, persisting patterns of dynamic energy with an inner sense of direction that know how to sustain themselves, grow, and evolve. In tune with the inner direction of the universe itself, they constantly create new relationships that add to the store of increasing complexity and "information." They create people, too.

We Make Ourselves and Others

The dynamic, co-creative relationship between the observer and the observed revealed by quantum physics means that when we are creating new realities by interacting with potentiality, we are creating new features of ourselves at the same time. Reality creation is a mutual, two-way process. The Chinese have always understood this. When their landscape painters "enter into a sympathetic unity" with a natural scene they are painting, they assume that in the creative act of producing their art, they are at the same time creating themselves. This was expressed by the poetess Kuang Chung-chi when she wrote,

> Whatsoever in thee good in nature
> Is carved into me;
> And all I have, sweet and pure,
> Will be osmosed into thee.[3]

Every time we seek new understanding by asking a probing question, do an experiment while working on an innovation, make a big decision, or act on an intuition, we are both creating new "answers" (remember Heisenberg?) and creating new neural pathways in our own brains. Those new neural

The Higher Meaning of Leadership & Companies   37

pathways in turn lead to changes in our personalities, character, and abilities, even to our health. Studies have discovered that 50% of who we are is determined by the genes we have inherited, but the remaining 50% forms and reforms over the years as we experience life. We are, to a significant extent, the authors of ourselves as we go about our daily lives choosing what to learn, what to explore, how to respond to life's challenges and opportunities, how or whether to discipline the many instinctual temptations arising from our lower brains (our "animal instincts"). The Chinese philosophers realised this through experience and intuition and that was why they so strongly advocated questioning, self-discipline, and lifelong self-cultivation as an aspirational path to sagehood. In my case, drawing my inspiration from the wider implications of quantum science, I have advocated these same ideals for the quantum leader.

We also, of course, create ourselves, and are created by, the relationships we form. We saw in Chapter 1 that relationships are what make all reality in our universe. Whenever two quantum entities come together in a relationship, something new is created, something new that is larger than the sum of its parts (quantum "emergence"). Similarly, whenever two people form a relationship, each of them displays or develops personal characteristics or behaviour distinctive of that relationship. In a different relationship, they become "different people." To a very great extent, we *are* our relationships, and our relationships then create further reality. In our quantum universe, new entities are always greater than the sum of their parts. That is why individuals caught up in a crowd exhibit a "crowd behaviour" unlike anything they would ever do as individuals. And it is why organisations like companies that harbour so many relationships can have "brains" and personalities "that function above and beyond the actions and decisions of their individual members," as Lord Stone observed about Marks & Spencer. But change the nature of those relationships that make up the company, the company will have a different "brain," leading to a different performance. There is an important lesson in this for leaders. Companies don't just create products, services, and themselves. Through the relationships and culture that exist in companies, they also create the people working within them.

I was walking one evening in Hangzhou with my friend Chen Feng, the founder and CEO of Tian Jian Water, a company that is fast becoming one of China's largest water treatment companies. Chen Feng asked me, "What do you think is my product?"

"Water, of course," I replied.

"No," he said, "My product is people. I want to build the 'Tian Jian person,' and I want the Tian Jian person to be a model for all of China's business community." He calls the company culture he is building "the Gentleman culture." The idea comes from the ideal of the Confucian Gentleman who engages in lifelong learning and self-cultivation, better to serve society and to be a more effective bridge between Heaven and Earth. Chen hopes the Tian Jian person will be a bridge between the old China and the new.

All new Tian Jian employees are put through a three-day training/induction programme to familiarise them with the company culture and what is expected of them. They are told that the company values stress learning and service. The programme includes some teachings from the *I Ching*, such as, "The highest excellence is that of water." This stresses that, like water, which flows freely and adapts its course to the obstacles in its path, the employees and their work practices must be flexible and adaptive. The company's name, *Tian Jian*, is taken from the first two characters in the *I Ching*, meaning "heaven/sky" and "energetically." The third character meaning "living/operating" is implied. I.e. this is a company driven by the energy of innovation and action, ultimately, as an energetic partner in heaven's (universal) creation.

To encourage learning and self-cultivation, there is an Isle of Learning, a very long corridor filled with recommended books, at Tian Jian company headquarters. To encourage good character, new employees are told that interdepartmental and intradepartmental cliques and conspiracies, and lies and cover-ups with bosses and customers, will not be tolerated. All are very common in China's less well-managed industries. Each employee is taught that the whole (the company, the team) is greater than the sum of its parts, and that each individual is responsible for the whole. They are also taught that at Tian Jian Water, the customer is the true boss and that "The ultimate goal of management is to manage myself." And they are inducted into the company's culture of constant and open questioning. "To ask questions is the most important ability," says Chen Feng. "It is important to ask questions of those with whom you disagree, not just with those whom you agree." He encourages his employees to question him.

Tian Jian Water is a happy, friendly company where human relationships are nurtured and treasured. Chen Feng himself is much loved for his habit of visiting sick employees in the hospital and personally greeting visiting parents from rural districts at the station. "He is our father and our brother," one employee told me. One of his senior vice presidents added, "I feel safe here. Whatever difficulties, I feel safe and supported, because the company is always backing me."

Chen Feng is a quantum leader. He cares about his people and nurtures their potential. He treats them with friendliness and respect, and trusts them with the freedom to make decisions, deal directly with customers, and to self-organise their work. He pays them well. He is mindful that positive motivation and a sense of purpose – helping to build the new China and participating in the work of heaven, no less! – will keep company energy levels high, and he manages in a way that energy flows freely through the company, just as water flows freely around the obstacles in its course. The result is a happy and productive workforce and an innovative company.

Business leaders like Chen Feng are too rare. Far too many, the vast majority, lead old paradigm companies that are soulless and impersonal, in which bureaucracy inhibits relationships and blocks the flow of energy, in which employee potential is wasted because people are heavily controlled from the top and expected simply to follow instructions and do what they are told. Questions and employee thinking are discouraged, mistakes are punished and thus experimentation stifled, bosses are rewarded with bonuses and workers underpaid, and workers are dismissed as simply instruments of production and shareholder value, replaceable parts in the corporate machine. Employees in these companies find no meaning or purpose in their work, feel disrespected, and often suffer abuse and humiliation from bullying bosses, and, as a result, are unhappy and unmotivated. They come to work simply because they have to earn a living somewhere. The result is a culture of fear, frequent absence due to illness, rapid employee turnover, low productivity, and less innovation – damaged and wasted people, and wasted potential. These companies may enjoy short-term success as measured by their bottom-line profit margins, but they destroy their own sustainability and creative evolution. Most Fortune 500 companies have a lifespan of five years. This old-paradigm top-down management is surely irresponsible management, cosmically irresponsible.

Responsible for the World

We create new reality, we create ourselves and others, we create the world. This offers purpose and meaning, and perhaps inspiration and even aspiration, to all our lives. But it also demands responsibility from each of us. We are responsible for the realities we create. We are responsible to make ourselves the best people we can be and to live lives that do not waste our potential. We are responsible for others and for building relationships with them that bring out the best in both them and ourselves. We are responsible for the world, for ensuring that our lives make a difference, that in some way, however large or small, they make the world a better place. This responsibility is borne by every human being.

Each one of us, in the course of our lives, brings something or someone (our children, the products of our labour) new into the world, each one of us uses our free will to make choices and to exhibit behaviour that affects ourselves and others, and each one of us creates a "world" for ourselves, the whole array of things, activities, people, events, etc. that frame our overall personal experience of living. And because everything is connected to everything, and everything is a part of everything else, these personal 'worlds' that each of us builds are a constituent part of that whole larger reality we call "*the* world." So each one of us contributes to creating the world and thus bears responsibility for the world.

But the scale on which companies create new realities and shape existing ones confers an even greater responsibility on business leaders. These leaders build companies that manufacture or produce products or create services that touch and influence the lives of every person in the world and, in many cases, that affect the environment, the planet, and even the likelihood or not that life on Earth will continue to be possible. Company leaders employ and determine the work and living conditions of the majority of people who live on Earth. These determine how much human potential is fulfilled or wasted. Their companies create the jobs and build the wealth that societies and economies need to function. Their innovations transform quantum potentiality into daily reality. Their wealth and power give them influence with governments and, in turn, influence policy decisions that affect virtually everyone and everything. These leaders and their companies create the world on a large scale, and their innovations and employment practices shape the cosmos.

During the thousands of years of imperial China, the emperor was believed to rule the people and "all under heaven" with a Mandate of Heaven, his authority sanctioned by heaven itself. But this Mandate was a *mutual* contract. In exchange for his power, the emperor had a duty to heaven to take good care of the people and all affected by his rule. If he failed in this duty, he was deemed to have lost his Mandate, and the people had the right to rise up against him. Many times in Chinese history, bad emperors did lose their Mandate. The people rose up, replaced him, and a new ruling dynasty was formed.

The physics of our quantum universe has conferred on us all, as human beings, a kind of Mandate of Heaven with similarly binding mutual conditions. We have been given the power to create the world, but in exchange, we are its stewards and guardians. If we create things, relationships, or circumstances that damage others or the world itself, those or that we have failed will rise up against us. These might be consumers or employees who rise up against the products or services or employment practices of companies and whose rebellion ends the rule of a CEO, the existence of a company, or even the dominance of business itself. In the case of the Earth, the damage our creations have been inflicting is already causing its climate changes to rise up against us. If we don't correct our behaviour quickly, this uprising will bring an end to our human "dynastic rule" – our civilisation, perhaps our existence as a species. The opportunities of our assigned role in the cosmos are awesome, but so are its responsibilities, and the consequences of how we bear that responsibility of cosmic significance. China's philosophers tell us we must make ourselves worthy. As the great contemporary philosopher Tu Wei-Ming expresses this task,

> The precondition for us to participate in the internal resonance of the vital forces in nature is our own inner transformation. Unless we can first harmonize our own feelings and thoughts, we are not prepared for nature, let alone for an "interflow with the spirit of Heaven and Earth." It is true that we are one with nature. But as humans, we must make ourselves worthy of such a relationship.[4]

Notes

1 Thome H. Fang, *The Chinese View of Life*, 78–83.
2 Rilke, "Letter to Hulewicz."
3 Quoted in Thome H. Fang, *The Chinese View of Life*, 140.
4 Tu Wei-Ming, *Confucian Thought*, 9.

4 The Mind of the Leader

Whatever the final and complete understanding of the relationship between consciousness and the full range of our human mental abilities and experience, the brain unquestionably plays a key role in connecting us to the world around us and in shaping that world as we know it. The importance of this for leaders is that, if they understand the capacities of their own brains, and how to get the best out of them, they will gain invaluable wisdom about how best to lead their companies and to be good quantum leaders themselves. Let us look at the mind, brain, thinking connection here as currently understood by the latest neuroscience.

We have just seen that companies, like all living systems, best function if they are enabled to perform as complex adaptive systems (CADs). But for most companies, this presents a strong restructuring and leadership challenge. Leaders will have to make a paradigm shift and change the thinking behind their thinking. They must first become aware that they have been acting under the influence of an outdated paradigm and understand how this has been affecting their management practices and company performance. Then they must get to a point where they can *feel* the reality of an alternative paradigm, feel the reality of thinking in a new way. Quantum Management argues that it is the new paradigm defined so clearly by the discoveries of quantum physics that best equips us to deal with the challenges and opportunities of 21st-century life, and I have called the new thinking that follows from the quantum paradigm "quantum thinking." But this raises several questions.

Modern science has made us aware that it is our brains that enable all thinking, and the way we use our brains influences the kind and quality of the thinking that we do. Quantum thinking allows us to deal more effectively with uncertainty, complexity, and rapid change. It enables the new insights and creative breakthroughs that lead to innovation. But how do our brains do quantum thinking, and how can we encourage more of it? Why have the Chinese found it natural to think "quantum" for thousands of years, while most people in the West find it so difficult? All people have the same brains, so do Chinese people and Western people use their brains differently? And can Western people do anything to make our thinking more quantum?

Three Kinds of Thinking

The brain is nature's most complex and multifaceted organisation. It is flexible, adaptive, and constantly rewires itself. All man-made organisations are in fact reflections of this natural template. Man-made organisations are approximations to the real thing based on their leaders' ability to draw on the full resources of nature's potential. If leaders deepen their understanding of this potential – if they raise their own awareness of brain dynamics, structure, and capacity – they will be better placed to rewire the corporate brains of the companies they lead.

The human brain is capable of three distinctive kinds of thinking. Rational, logical, rule-bound thinking produces concepts and categories similar to those in Western logic and the Newtonian paradigm. Associative, more habit-bound thinking, more developed in East Asian cultures, gives us our pattern-recognising abilities, an ability to deal with paradox and ambiguity, and is getting closer to features of the quantum paradigm – everything is interlinked. The third kind of thinking is creative, rule-breaking, and rule-making thinking gives us intuitive insight and the "aha!" experience of sudden new discovery and behaves very like the emergent structures found in the quantum paradigm. Today's neuroscience tells us that these three kinds of thinking each relies on different neural structures or processes in the brain and that these structures and processes are largely different in the brain's two hemispheres.

Serial Thinking

Our simplistic model of "thinking" as something straightforward, logical, and dispassionate is not wrong. It is just part of the story. It is a model derived from formal logic and arithmetic – "If x then y" or "2+2=4." This kind of thinking is logical, rational, and rule-bound. It separates and isolates data to enable focus, concentration, and analysis. It breaks experience apart. It solves problems by step-by-step, serial reasoning, breaking them down into their simplest parts. It is goal-directed, instrumental, and objective. When thinking this way, we stand back from, or distance ourselves from, experience and *objectify* it. And then we build mental models that help us handle future such experiences in a predictable, confident way. Each time an event happens that matches our mental model, the neural wiring that controls our response strengthens. The brain's ability to do serial thinking is enabled by a kind of neural wiring called *neural tracts*.

Neural tracts are neurons connected one-on-one in a series, like a series of telephone cables. The head of one neuron connects to the tail of the next one, and an electrochemical signal passes along the chain of linked neurons being employed for any particular thought or series of thoughts. Each neuron is switched either on or off, and if any neuron in the chain gets damaged or switched off, the whole chain ceases to function, like a chain of Christmas tree lights wired serially. This kind of wiring predominates in the brain's left hemisphere and is the kind of wiring used in PCs. The left brain is, effectively, a computing machine. All human beings can do serial thinking more or less well, but PCs are even better at it, being both faster and more accurate.

Like the kind of thinking that arises from the paradigm of Newtonian physics, both the structures and thinking produced by neural tracts are linear, deterministic, and atomistic. B always follows A in the same way. Serial thinking does not tolerate nuance or ambiguity. It is strictly on/off, black-and-white, either/or thinking. Hugely effective within its set of rules (its program) and learned expectations, the serial thinking process breaks down if someone moves the goal posts or presents it with something unexpected. It is like a PC asked to do a task not in its program. In that case, a message flashes on the screen to tell us "system not operating." It is finite thinking that operates within boundaries and likes routine. It is of no use when we need to scan the horizon for possibilities or when we have to deal with the unexpected.

A great deal of the thinking involved in management-as-usual is serial thinking. The analysis phase of an enterprise relies on breaking the problem or situation we are facing down into its simplest logical parts and then noticing or predicting the consequences of decisions that have been made in the past or that we are making now. Most strategic planning done with this kind of thinking assumes a game plan and a step-by-step rationale for enacting it. "Management by objectives" assumes we set clear goals and objectives and work out a logical series of actions for achieving them. Similarly, most education being offered to the vast majority of students in schools all over the world has increasingly become "education by objectives." Students are presented with clear learning goals they are meant to achieve by school leaving age, teachers are instructed to present them with the knowledge available to achieve these goals, and their success in doing so is objectively measured by exam results.

Traditional Taylorian companies have many structures in place that embody serial thinking. The eight-hour shift itself, the time clock that signs employees in and out, the siloed job descriptions and codes of dress, the whole bureaucratic structure describing responsibilities, codes of practice, holiday schedules, coffee breaks, and sickness benefits – all these are defined by rules applying to everyone in a set category. Serial thinking underlies the factory-floor blueprint or the engineer's repair manual. All serial thinking assumes the corporate world consists of parts (people, nuts and bolts, markets, customers, competitors) who can be manipulated successfully through rules and five-year plans because they are themselves predictable in their behaviour, just as the deterministic Newtonian universe is governed by immutable Laws of Nature. In the same way, the standard school day is organised on a set schedule, the required curriculum provides a blueprint for achieving desired objectives, the learning experience is divided into separate, siloed subject matter (separate parts), and all students are expected to learn the same material in the same way. Universally applied school rules, and usually school dress codes, are meant to ensure predictable results.

The advantages of machine-like serial thinking are that it is efficient – fast, accurate, precise, and reliable. The chief disadvantage is that it can only operate within a given program or set of rules – in an orderly, predictable, controllable world. Similarly, the advantage of serial structures in organisations is that they are efficient, reliable, and universal. But the disadvantage is that they are inflexible. They do not adapt, they cannot respond to exceptions, rapid change, the unexpected, or "mess." And they rely totally for their design and function on *already known* facts and realities. They do not cope well with 21st-century realities and today's need for constant innovation and the creative, exploratory, experimentation and thinking that makes it possible. Western cultures, and those Asian companies and schools that have adopted Western organisational and learning models in the hope of "modernising to catch up," are left-brain dominated. But many of the issues that move people to speak of a "decline of the West" can be traced to the inadequacy of Western reliance on serial thinking and on the cultural, organisational, and strategic practices and structures that follow from it.

Associative, Networked Thinking

A second kind of thinking we can do is associative or parallel thinking. This kind of thinking, which focuses heavily on the *relationship* between things and events in our experience, helps us develop effective responses and strategies between things like hunger and food that will satisfy it, between the need for reassurance and any compliments or praise we may receive, between the colour red and emotions of excitement or danger. Associative thinking also enables us to recognise patterns like faces or smells and to learn bodily skills like riding a bicycle or driving a car.

The neural structures within the brain with which we do associative thinking are known as *neural networks,* and these predominate in the right hemisphere of the brain. Each of these networks contains bundles of up to a hundred thousand neurons, and each single neuron in a bundle may be connected to as many as a thousand others. The connections themselves are random, messy, or parallel – that is, each neuron acts upon or is acted upon by many others, simultaneously. And the neural networks in the brain are connected to further neural networks located throughout the brain and the body. Thus, the intelligence we gain from right-brain experience is embodied, emotionally informed intelligence. China's great philosophers never spoke of "mind" as an independent function or entity, but always of "heart-mind," believing that our mental life is always informed and influenced by matters of the heart. Associative thinking could be thought of as the "brain's heart."

Unlike the right brain's serial neural tracts, neural networks have the ability to wire and rewire themselves in dialogue with experience. Each time we see a pattern, the neural networks that recognise it grow stronger, until recognition becomes automatic. If the pattern alters, our ability to perceive it will slowly alter, too, until the brain has rewired itself easily to recognise the new pattern.

When we first learn to drive a car, for instance, every move of our hands and feet is consciously deliberate, and our control of the car is only slight. With each practice driving session, however, needed coordination between hands, feet, and brain is more strongly wired into the brain's neural networks (their interconnections grow stronger) until, eventually, we don't think about our driving at all unless there is some unusual problem. Indeed, it even becomes *impossible* to think consciously, or at least easily, about our driving skills. When my then 12-year-old son asked me, "Mum, what foot do you use to press the clutch pedal?" I couldn't answer him. I had to get behind the wheel of the car and *watch* my left foot go down on the clutch. My foot knew how to work the clutch, but my conscious mind had 'forgotten' this!

All associative learning is trial-and-error learning. When a rat learns to run a maze, it doesn't follow rules, it *practices*. If a trial run fails, no neural connections are wired in; if it succeeds, the rat's brain strengthens the relevant connections. This kind of learning is heavily experience-based. It is also habit-bound – the more times I perform a skill successfully, the more inclined I will be to do it that way next time. Associative learning is also *tacit* learning – we learn a skill, but can't articulate any rules or steps by which we learned it. Neural networks are not connected with our language faculty, nor with our ability to articulate concepts. We *feel* our skills, we *perform* our skills, we *embody* them, but we don't think or talk about them.

A great deal of the knowledge possessed by a company is tacit knowledge, knowledge which no one can frame or articulate but upon which the company relies for its lifeblood. This tacit knowledge is embedded in the skills and experience of the company's leaders and employees, and it is lost if these skilled, experienced employees leave the company. Frequent leadership or employee turnover seriously drains a company's knowledge capital. This is one reason why looking after and considering the needs of its employees is in a company's self-interest. Happy, well-paid employees who find a sense of meaning and purpose in their work are loyal employees.

The advantages of associative thinking are that it is in dialogue with experience and can learn through trial and error as it goes along. It can feel its way in untried situations and respond and adapt to unexpected events or challenges. It is also a kind of thinking that can handle nuance and ambiguity. Up to 80% of a given pattern may be missing, but the neural networks can recognise what is left. There have been computers modelled on neural networks, sometimes known as parallel processors, that are used to discriminate tastes and smells, for facial recognition, to recognise handwriting and be able to read things like postal codes. A parallel processor can recognise a postal code written in millions of different samples of handwriting. The disadvantages of associative thinking are that it is slow, it can be inaccurate, and much of it tends to be habit-bound. We *can* reskill, break or change a bad habit, but it takes time and effort. And because associative thinking is tacit thinking and creates tacit knowledge, we have difficulty sharing it with others. We can't just write out a formula and tell another to get on with the job. Each of us must learn a skill in our own way, for ourselves. No two brains have the same set of neural connections.

Creative, "Quantum" Thinking

A third kind of thinking that we do is creative, insightful, and intuitive thinking. It is the kind of thinking with which we challenge our assumptions, break our habits, or change our mental models, our paradigms. It is the kind of thinking that invents new categories of thought, that sees patterns and relationships never before known to have existed and, of course, the kind of thinking that leads to innovative breakthroughs. This kind of thinking is also rooted in and motivated by a deep sense of meaning and value. It is also rooted in our lived sense of our bodies and has a significant input from the brain's emotional centre.

Over the years, many top scientists like David Bohm and Roger Penrose have suggested that such creative and intuitive thinking, consciousness itself, is made possible by quantum activity in or a quantum field across the brain. And recent discoveries of quantum biology have certainly shown that cell communication, both throughout the body and in the brain, is partly enabled by quantum coherence, quantum tunnelling, quantum resonance, and quantum non-locality.[1] Many others, including myself, have suggested that the 40 Hz or "gamma field" that sweeps across the brain during all conscious activity may itself be a quantum field.[2] But while any such proven quantum activity remains fertile ground for further exploration and more deep understanding of our higher mental life, these suggestions about "quantum consciousness" are still, at this stage, grounded speculation.

More definitely, like the associative thinking just described, creative, intuitive thinking is associated with the right brain's neural networks and is certainly facilitated by the *complexity* created by countless relationships and interconnections between vast numbers of these networks. Such complexity generates *emergent*, new realities, such as the unique properties and behaviour of living systems. The brain is, of course, a complex adaptive system (CAD), and in CADs, it is the system complexity of these relationships that makes them living quantum systems. We have seen that in quantum physics, relationship gives rise to new reality. The "new reality" arising from the right brain's relational complexity takes the form of intuitive understanding, new insights, and creative, breakthrough thought. This is the kind of thinking needed for innovation. I call it "quantum thinking" because its capacities and processes, like all those of CADs, are very like those first described by quantum physics.

Similarly, the new AI systems that are now rapidly, and radically, changing nearly every aspect of both our daily and professional lives have been made possible by drawing on the many creative potentials of this complexity. The very earliest AI models drew their inspiration from the work of "connectionist" philosophers who were themselves exploring the creative implications of the right brain's neural networks. Existing AI systems cannot yet entirely mimic human creativity but, while it is still debatable whether they can ever justifiably be said to possess something like full human consciousness and self-awareness, it is only a matter of time before they will not just equal but exceed the capacities of human intelligence. But it will always be the minds, motives, purposes, and values, as well as the character of the humans programming the algorithms that guide these AI "super brains" that determine whether their superintelligence is used for good or ill. If we "mere humans" are to form intelligent partnerships of positive benefit with the AI machines, we must increase our own capacity for quantum thinking and its associated quantum leadership qualities, qualities the ancient Chinese described as those of a "sage." Here, we will briefly remind ourselves of practices that cultivate the creative aspects of quantum thinking. In the next chapter, we will look at the broader question of cultivating quantum leadership character or sagehood.

Cultivating Quantum Thinking

The quantum-like features of our thinking that enable us to have new insights and think out of the box arise from the brain's complexity, which in turn emerges from relationships within and between the right brain's neural networks. These neural relationships underpin our ability to make conscious mental associations between one thing and another. Thus, becoming more conscious of existing and possible relationships helps us better apply quantum thinking in both our strategic and innovative thinking. Some of these relationships to become more conscious of are simply in our surrounding environment, the people and things that influence us and make us who we are, and those people and things influenced by us. In our personal lives, these are family and friends, people we meet and the material "tools" we use in our daily lives. In our business lives, they are our work associates or employees, our customers, our partners, and our competitors. And then there are also, of course, our relationships with features of the surrounding physical environment, like geography and climate, and events in the geopolitical environment. Other relationships it is creative to become more conscious of are those held in the vast storehouse of our unconscious minds and perhaps in the collective unconscious of humanity at large. And then, of course, there are relationships with Nature and the universe itself that are simply embedded in our biological and physical bodies. Different practices and habits we can adopt or cultivate help to increase the creative potential of seeing and building relationships.

- Simple Awareness. Many of us go through much of the day "lost in thought," preoccupied with what we are trying to accomplish or what we are planning to do next, or drifting off into imagination or fantasy. We simply don't notice our surroundings, and we miss a great deal. Developing a conscious habit of observing and paying some attention to what is "right before our eyes" can strengthen our relationship to our immediate surroundings, natural, physical, and human.

- Sitting With, and Asking More, Questions. We saw earlier that when a quantum scientist asks a question or conducts an experiment, he/she is dropping a bucket into the vast well of unknown quantum potentiality and bringing up a bucketful of new, actualised reality – a new understanding of or perspective on the nature of some way our universe works. In the same way, the questions we ask ourselves and others during the day bring up bucketfuls of new knowledge or understanding that challenge our assumptions, change our perspectives, and give us new, innovative ideas. We can never ask too many questions. And there are no "foolish questions." If leaders encourage a questioning culture in their companies, urging employees to share questions among themselves, and feel free to question their superiors, and even the CEO himself, these companies will be happier and more fear-free, more unified and cooperative, and more innovative.

  And then, whether we call it reflection, reflective practice, or meditation, making time at the beginning or end of our usually busy days to sit alone quietly, and just let our minds dwell on questions, drops buckets into the vast well of our unconscious minds. Psychologists now tell us that 90% of our brain's mental activity is unconscious. During our entire waking day, we see, hear, and experience things that we simply don't consciously notice. This is because the brain is designed to filter out incoming information (data) that is not immediately relevant to accomplishing tasks or solving problems of immediate concern. That "extraneous" information gets stored in the unconscious. Later, when sitting quietly, if we focus our thoughts on deeper questions related to those tasks or problems, that wealth of unconscious knowledge delivers up new answers or solutions or guides us to use a search engine like Google to find them. Similarly, when sitting quietly, entirely new questions may spontaneously occur to us that lead us to see relationships or associations we, and perhaps no one else, had ever considered. We experience these new answers or understanding they "bring up" as "creative insights."

- Time Out, Time Off: Business-as-usual management practices usually demand that employees be at their desks, with their minds fully focused on the work assigned throughout the working day, and very commonly even for hours during the evening or weekend, either at home or with extra time present in the office. Employees are scolded or punished if caught chatting to workmates, reading something unrelated to their jobs, or simply "gazing into space." Yet it is well known to psychologists that it is when taking a break, taking our minds off a problem or work demand, that a solution or new insight occurs to us. This is because, when allowed freedom from the demands of focused attention, the brain has more energy to access all the many relationships and associations stored in the unconscious. Knowing the creative potential of such time out or time off is one reason Japanese businessmen often break for a round of golf and why Japanese office workers try not to disturb colleagues when they appear to be "doing nothing." And in Silicon Valley tech companies, which are more likely to be managed in a "quantum" way, it is the custom for employees to take breaks of one kind or another during the working day, and for the working day itself to be much more loosely structured.

- Dialogue: In his later years, David Bohm devoted much of his time to thinking and writing about dialogue and to establishing dialogue groups. He referred to dialogue as "quantum conversation" because of its creative potential to challenge people's assumptions, free them from stuck and restrictive mental models, and lead participants to collective, new understanding or insights. The origins of dialogue go back to ancient Greece and the teaching methods of Socrates. The essence of a dialogue conversation is that it is question-led and exploratory, based on asking questions rather than giving answers, "finding out" rather than "knowing," listening to others and together exploring new possibilities rather than proving a point or defending an argument or position of one's own. When engaged in dialogue, all people are considered equal and their contributions worth listening to. There is no status hierarchy. And participants show respect for one another rather than trying to gain power over them. Dialogue groups always result in lessening tension and unproductive animosity between opposing parties and a more shared respect for each other's points of view, and very often to creative group breakthroughs. Again, this is simply because opening the mind to free exploration and enquiry allows the brain to discover or create new mental associations.

- Exposure to Diversity: One of the best ways to encourage "thinking out of the box" and encourage our minds to see or make new associations is of course simply to expose ourselves to more diverse experiences – reading widely outside our specialised field of interest, making friends with people from different cultures, travelling to new and different places, listening to music and attending the theatre, looking at practices and skills in industries very different from our own. Some innovative companies ensure employee access to such diversity by offering after-work programmes that bring in artists, writers, philosophers, musicians, theatre people, or lectures by people from other industries.

To sum up the value of all these various practices, I repeat: Quantum physics teaches us that new relationships create new reality. New mental associations create new insights and thus innovation.

Can the Brain Give Us "Cosmic Consciousness"?

The Chinese have always assumed a natural capacity of the human mind to be in tune with, or to function in a similar way to, the principles according to which the universe functions. Zhang Zai tells us, "By enlarging one's mind, one can enter into all the things in the world [to examine and understand their principle]."[3] He calls this quality of mind/cosmic "resonance" *ganying* and credits it with man's capacity to live according to *Dao*. Indeed, as we have seen, this resonance (*gan*) between human nature (*renxing*), both mental and bodily, and the nature of both cosmic reality and living Nature underpins the whole basis of Chinese thought and the Chinese worldview. It is the basis of *I Ching* thought and is expressed in the early, and foundational, concept of *Tian Ren Heyi*, "the alignment of Heaven, Man, and Earth." It is also the basis of the *Liangzhi*, or "moral intuition," that shapes so much of Wang Yangming's teaching. Man, having this natural alignment, *ganying* or *Liangzhi*, with the Way of Heaven, is the bridge between Heaven and Earth and bears the responsibility of bringing the Way of Heaven to all his projects and relationships here on Earth. Indeed, as we have seen, in the Chinese worldview, fulfilling this responsibility is the *purpose* of human life. The whole of Confucian thought, with its emphasis on self-cultivation and appropriate conduct, is devoted to instructing us on how to fulfil this purpose of our existence.

The philosophy that David Bohm and other quantum philosophers like myself have extracted from the defining principles of quantum physics describes a similar worldview based on this same co-creative relationship between the human mind, Nature, and the way of our quantum universe. This quantum worldview arises in part simply because quantum science has demonstrated that we human beings are fully part of Nature and the universe, stuff of the same substance. Additionally, as I wrote above, Bohm, Roger Penrose, myself, and others have wondered whether such Mind/Nature/Universe alignment, or "cosmic consciousness," could arise from quantum activity in, or a possible quantum field across, the brain that resonates in some way with the physical laws of our quantum universe. Such speculation has occurred to modern Western thinkers in other fields.

The great Swiss psychologist Karl Jung suggested that the mysterious synchronicity between events happening in different times or places, or the ability of an *I Ching* consultation to give a meaningful and appropriate "answer" to a question being asked, might be enabled by some form of quantum resonance between the brain and an outside field of shared information. This speculation underpinned his famous idea of "the collective unconscious" and was the same thought behind David Bohm's saying,

> If you reach deeply into yourself, you are reaching the very essence of mankind. When you do this, you will be led into the generating depth

of consciousness that is common to the whole of mankind and that has the whole of mankind enfolded in it. The individual's ability to be sensitive to that becomes the key to the change of mankind. We are all connected. If this could be taught, and if people could understand it, we would have a different consciousness.[4]

Similar suggestions of a quantum resonance between the brain and things or events external to it have been proposed to explain ESP, or extra-sensory phenomena, like telepathy, precognition, and remote viewing[5] – all subjects of interest and research by military and intelligence agencies in America, China, Russia, and other countries. The possibility that our brains might actually experience this resonance is strengthened both by the proven phenomena of quantum non-locality ("action at a distance") between elementary particles like photons and by quantum resonance associated with quantum physical systems and cell communication in biological systems. It is certainly the case that a quantum information field permeates the entire universe. If it is finally proven that a quantum field across the human brain can resonate with this cosmic information field, it would offer contemporary scientific credibility to the early Chinese assumption that *ganying* and *Liangzhi* really do exist and that they enable a "cosmic consciousness" that aligns human intelligence with the Way of the universe.

Notes

1 Jim Al-Khalili and Johnjoe McFadden, *Life on the Edge*.
2 Danah Zohar, *SQ: Spiritual Intelligence*.
3 Quoted in Wing-Tsit Chan, *A Sourcebook in Chinese Philosophy*, 515.
4 Quoted in Joseph Jaworski, *The Inner Path to Leadership*, 80.
5 See, for instance, Danah Zohar, *Through the Time Barrier*.

Part II
The Quantum/Chinese Leader

5 The Quantum Leader as a Modern Sage King

We have seen that companies can play an important creative role in society and in the universe itself, but if they are to do so, they must have great leaders. Here, I want to explore the qualities a quantum leader would possess.

A leader, of course, is a person of action. Leaders make things happen. But not all actions are good actions, and things that happen often bring about bad consequences. Personally, I believe that most of the crises facing our world today are being caused by, or made worse, either because our leaders have chosen to neglect big problems, are too incompetent to solve them, or are making bad decisions leading to destructive consequences. I believe that our world is in crisis because we have a leadership crisis. This is true in both national and global affairs and in business. I will concentrate on the crisis in business leadership.

In 2019, Gallup did a survey that indicated bad leadership had cost US companies at least $960 billion per year. But that is only the cost measured in money and only the cost to these companies' "bottom line." The cost to customers and to society in general is greater. As consumers, we are all dependent on companies providing the products and services that we need. As citizens, we rely on companies to provide the jobs we need and to generate much of the tax revenue that pays for our public services. And the cost of this bad leadership to employees is immeasurable. The soul of any company is found in its people, in the pride they take in their work, and the meaning and sense of purpose they might gain from it. But I have spoken with so many very intelligent young people working in companies who describe the frustration and depression they feel because bad managers interfere with their ability to do their jobs well.

In his own comments about management at Haier, Zhang Ruimin says,

> The same set of employee policies and procedures can enable employees to be fully functional at work if followed by managers in a good way, but cause all kinds of difficulties for employees if implemented by managers in a bad way. A manager imposing orders or a penalty on an employee is doing good if his intention is to help the employee's work change for

the better, but they are doing considerable harm if the intention is only to demonstrate or impose their own authority on them.

Too many managers are too keen to demonstrate their authority in order to reassure themselves of their own importance. Sadly, some are just bullies.

The challenges and demands of management are changing. They are more nuanced and complex. Today's leaders must deal with uncertainty, often chaos, rapid change, and global interconnectivity. They must deal with employees who are often better educated, who are seeking different returns from their work, and who may be drawn from a variety of backgrounds and cultures. Employee attitudes towards authority and personal empowerment are changing, and customer expectations are also more varied and demanding. The very nature of management is changing, and this will require not just a new management paradigm but also, not just *better* leaders, a new *kind* of leader. I have called them "quantum leaders" and written about them at length,[1] but in the spirit of this book, I feel we can gain a deeper understanding of what it fully means to be a quantum leader by also looking at what China's great philosophers had to say about the ideal leader.

The *I Ching* offers extensive advice about the qualities and wisest possible decisions for leaders, and just as Quantum Management argues that quantum leadership and quantum thinking are matters of deep personal commitment, attitude, and practice, the *I Ching* counsels might aspire to leadership first be certain they have a true calling for the role and the qualities that make them equal to the task:

> What is required [in society] is that we unite with others, in order that all may complement and aid one another through working together. But such a [working] together calls for a central figure around whom other persons may unite. To become a center of influence holding people together is a grave matter and fraught with responsibility. It requires greatness of spirit, consistency, and strength. Therefore, let him who wishes to gather others about him ask himself whether he is equal to the undertaking, for anyone attempting the task without a real calling for it only makes confusion worse than if no union at all had taken place.[2]

The Chinese notion of an ideal leader is called a sage-king, a person who can be sagely (wise) on the inside and kingly in the world of action. The original sage-kings who were models for the ideal were the three great leaders of antiquity, Yao, Shun, and Yu. The sage-king leadership ideal originates from the Confucian tradition and, like all things Confucian, is both quantum and non-quantum at the same time. Yao, Shun, and Yu were paternalistic and hierarchical, and their leadership authoritarian – definitely not a model for quantum leadership.

Quantum leaders give up most power, allowing their organisations and employees to self-organise. Foregoing top-down, directive leadership, they see themselves as a leader of leaders, who guide their companies with the authority of their character and personal example. Freed of controlling top-down commands and fierce oversight, employees fulfil more of their potential, are motivated to be more productive, and feel greater loyalty to their companies. Quantum leaders follow more the advice of Lao Tzu, "Rulers should rule as a chef cooks fish – lightly."

But the Confucian sage-king also devotes himself to lifelong moral self-cultivation, wide learning, and acquiring culture, and he brings these things to leadership that is wise, knowledgeable, and in service to both society and the people he leads. Yao, Shun and Yu possessed *ren*, or benevolence. They were kind and respectful to those they ruled, good-natured, and tried to build trust and good relationships in the kingdoms they ruled. Their moral integrity was without question. This made them beloved and respected by the people. All excellent models for the qualities of quantum leadership. Mencius summed up the wisdom of light-touch leadership in combination with these personal leadership qualities when he wrote, "When people submit to force, they do so not willingly but because they are fearful. When people submit to the transforming influence of morality, they do so sincerely, with admiration in their hearts."[3]

In the Confucian tradition, the sage-king is most often portrayed as a political leader, but many of China's great thinkers apply the term more broadly to the ideal leader in any sphere of society. The quantum leader, too, might be a political leader, but in Quantum Management Theory, I usually describe him/her as the leader of a company. In writing here, I will focus my remarks about both the sage-king and the quantum leader with business leaders in mind.

The Neo-Confucian philosophers who emphasised the notion of the sage-king, outlined several stages of development for a person to be worthy of being considered one:

- "Making illustrious virtue manifest": The sage-king must be "a person of virtue," a good person, naturally compassionate, and filled with benevolence – a wish to bring good to others. According to Song dynasty philosopher Zhou Dunyi,

The virtue of the sage is identical with that of heaven and earth: his brilliance is identical with that of the sun and the moon; his order is identical with that of the four seasons; and his fortunes and misfortunes are identical with those of spiritual beings.[4]

- And like the quantum leader, the sage-king cultivates his virtue so that he can help others to raise their moral standards and become good and compassionate people.

One's nature is the source of all things, and it is not one's own private possession. Therefore, when he establishes himself, he will help others establish themselves. He will share his knowledge with all. He will love universally. When he achieves something, he wants others to achieve the same.[5]

- "Unifying the will": As the Indian *Upanishads* say:

  > We are what our deep, driving desire is.
  > As our deep, driving desire is, so is our will.
  > As our will is, so is our deed.
  > As our deed is, so is our destiny.[6]

  To become a leader with the qualities of virtue and benevolence, the sage-king must "unify the will" or "purify the will." Some have interpreted this as to "strengthen the will," but Wang Yang Ming stresses that strengthening our will is not the point, but rather "transforming the will" so that it will work as a force for goodness within us. Just as I have pointed out in my work that "the quantum self" is a whole chorus of often conflicting sub-selves, or desires, emotions, and goals,[7] Wang Yang Ming and most other Chinese philosophers believed that, though human beings are essentially good, our nature carries within it instincts and desires that can lead us to do bad. Plato described the human self as a "chariot being pulled in different directions by the horses of divided will." To develop the best qualities latent within us, we must desire to be good, unify the will, and get all our horses to pull in the same direction.

  Most Western teachers have insisted that to make it our will to be good, we must follow laws prescribed by God, holy books, or religious leaders. Many Chinese philosophers believed we could turn our wills to good things by studying the Classics, the great founding books of the Chinese tradition. Confucius believed we could ensure our goodness by practising the "rituals," accepted social customs that act as a moral guide through our practising them. But Wang Yang Ming insisted that studying books and practising rituals were not necessary because all human beings possess innate moral intuition, or *liangzi* (pronounced *"Liangzhi"*), because of our natural resonance (*gangying*) with Heaven, the Way of the universe. The *Dao* itself is essentially good, so if we follow the *Dao*, we simply *know* what is good. I have taken this same position in describing "quantum morality," arguing that we carry within us the whole history and nature of the universe. The universe is poised towards the creation of ever more order and information, and it achieves this by constantly building new relationships. Quantum morality tells us that we are being good when we are forming ever-new, loving relationships.

- "Investigating things and extending knowledge": The early Neo-Confucian, Zhu Xi, emphasised "the investigation of things," the importance of looking deeply into the nature of things, to get to the bottom of them. In his commentary on *The Great* Learning, he says that all things, problems, events, have a defining principle within them that makes them what they are. If we wish to extend our knowledge to the utmost, we must investigate the principles of all things we come into contact with."[8] Likewise, the quantum leader should inquire deeply into things, not just take matters at face value, but look at the *origin* of problems and situations, and study the relationships at play. They should read widely and extensively, experience widely and extensively, and be a cultured person. But Wang Yang Ming's own particular twist on these matters is most close to the qualities of the sage-king and those I have associated with the quantum leader.

Wang Yang Ming stressed the importance of "knowledge in action," being both knowledgeable and actively engaging with matters and events in the world by putting one's knowledge into action. Knowledge without action, he said, is useless, and action without knowledge is dangerous. For the Chinese, any sage, wise man, is simply assumed to be a person of action. In the Chinese language itself, there is no distinction between knowing and acting in the very word used for "to know" or "knowledge." To know something is always to be making something happen, to be bringing something new into being (*realising* it). Just as in quantum physics, there is no distinction between the observer and what he/she observes. To observe a quantum entity, and thus to know whether it is a wave or a particle, is a co-creative dialogue between the observation being made and the quantum potentiality of that entity. By observing, knowing, the entity, the scientist transforms one of its potentialities into an actuality. They *realise* it. Just as a quantum company transforms potential products or services into new realities through the process of innovation.

Wang's prescription for engaging with things and thus acquiring knowledge is also very "quantum." He called upon leaders to *reflect* deeply on things, including reflecting deeply on one's self and one's behaviour, and to do so by much questioning, especially reflecting on and questioning their own assumptions. As the *I Ching* teaches, "It is only when we have the courage to face things exactly as they are, without any sort of self-deception or illusion, that a light will develop out of events, by which the path to success can be recognized."[9] It is constant self-examination and self-questioning that assures this. Heisenberg's Uncertainty Principle demonstrated that it is by questioning reality that the quantum scientist learns about reality. The sage-king and quantum leader, similarly, seek understanding through questioning, understanding of themselves and of worldly matters. Instead of seeking answers, they try to find the right question. Both would agree with the 20th-century Indian teacher Krishnamurti, who said, "By asking the right question sincerely, you have an *experience* of the answer – an inner understanding of the situation in question." This ability to experience answers by way of asking questions is powerfully expressed in Rilke's poem, "Live the Questions":

I beg you as much as I can to explore everything unknown in your heart. To love the questions themselves, as though they are locked rooms, or books written in a foreign tongue.

Do not seek the answers, because you would not be able to live them. And the point is to live everything.

So, live the questions now. And then, perhaps, in some distant day, you may live into the answer.

- "Regulating the family and ordering the state": We too often make a distinction between private life and public conduct and willingly accept that great leaders may be failed human beings. But Quantum Management insists this is a false dichotomy. To be a good leader, the quantum leader must be a good person in all spheres of their lives. Their personal life must be in order if their conduct of business is to be in order, so the priority in their development as a leader is first to develop themselves and their family relationships. Only then will they be ready to lead and be a moral example to others. This same order of priorities is outlined for the sage-king in *The Great Learning*:

  > One comes near the Way in knowing what to put first and what to put last. Those of antiquity who wished that all people throughout the empire would let their inborn virtue shine forth put governing their states well first; wishing to govern their states well, they first established harmony in their households; wishing to establish harmony in their households, they first cultivated themselves; wishing to cultivate themselves, they first put their minds in the right; wishing to first put their minds in the right, they first made their intentions true; wishing to make their intentions true, they first extended their knowledge to the utmost; the extension of knowledge lies in the investigation of things.[10]

  As Confucius says, "Once you have rectified yourself, you can serve in government without difficulty. But if you haven't rectified yourself, how can you rectify the people?" So much for the attitude in so many companies that it is quite a good thing if the CEO "is a bit of a bastard!" It is because their leaders are themselves driven by lower motivations like selfishness, greed, and arrogance that many companies harm, rather than serve, society. Yet Adam Smith built his model of capitalism on the very assumption that "People are selfish. They will always serve Number One." It is because these poor personal leadership qualities are sometimes even assumed as beneficial for success in the market that capitalism has been such a damaging social force in Western countries. It encourages craving and greed, and a willingness to trample on or take advantage of others to further one's own success. In China and several other Asian countries whose cultures stress service to others above selfish individualism, capitalism is usually accompanied, and transformed for the good of society, by more socialist values. We could transform the nature of capitalism everywhere were it to be accompanied by less selfish values.
- "Making the world tranquil": All organisations work best when there is harmony among all involved. We have seen that companies are energy systems, but for energy systems to be in balance, to be coherent, the energies of various parts and various members must be aligned, and the energies must be harmonious. Establishing such harmony is the central value of the sage-king, just as maintaining harmony and national unity is the primary

value in all Chinese thought and government. The American sinologist Stephen Angle says that sages have

> an active form of moral perception that I call 'looking for harmony' that explains both the sense in which their knowledge in action can be said to be unified and the resulting ease with which they can act…. And we see that a person striving towards sagehood should seek imaginative resolutions to moral conflicts that honor all relevant values.[11]

- This is true of not just moral conflicts but of all conflicts. The sage-king or quantum leader can resolve all conflicts by encouraging people to listen to and honour all points of view, to celebrate rather than feel threatened by diversity.

  One of my greatest personal reasons for appreciating my time in today's China is that it is such a united and harmonious society – a striking contrast with my daily life in the West. The freedom to express and demonstrate our differences is one of the precious qualities of democracy, but in our currently tragically polarised democracies, we seem to have lost our ability to resolve those differences. We have lost our ability to listen to each other. Life in the West today is not very happy. Quantum societies exist at the edge of chaos, neither too ordered to be creative nor too chaotic so as to tear themselves apart. Harmony in a quantum society assures a balance between unity on the one hand and a healthy public conversation debating all points of view on the other.

  In quantum companies, leaders often incorporate dialogue groups as a "safe place" where employees can express their grievances or conflicting views, "investigate things" through sincere, nonaggressive expression, creatively listen to one another, and thus resolve conflicts or learn to respect each other's positions, by getting to the *root* of their differences.

- "Cultivating the person": In laying out the would-be sage-king's development priorities in preparing for his public leadership, *The Great Learning* tells us that "cultivating the person" is the first and most important of these. And not just for leaders, but for all people: "Things have their roots and branches; affairs have a beginning and an end. From the Son of Heaven to the common people, all must regard cultivation of the personal life as the root and the foundation."[12] First, and the foundation, but not a one-off exercise undertaken early in life. Rather, as is true about the essential foundation of quantum leadership, self-cultivation is a constant, lifelong process. The quantum leader must be a quantum self, and becoming a quantum self takes a lifetime – perhaps many lifetimes.

  For the Chinese philosophers, self-cultivation is *moral* self-cultivation, the lifelong process of transforming our will so that it serves the better instincts and desires within our complex, many-faceted selves. "The sage had best to develop himself so that his influence may endure. He must make himself strong in every way by casting out what is inferior and degrading."[13] But for the Chinese, this moral self-cultivation is furthered by *cultural* self-cultivation, becoming a learned person by reading widely, experiencing and practising the arts – calligraphy, music, and poetry, as well as the martial arts, which cultivate discipline and align our personal energies with those of Heaven. Cultivation in these things also broadens the imagination and the range of creative associations the brain can make, thus fostering creativity and innovative thinking, "quantum thinking."

As I have said in describing the lifelong self-cultivation required for quantum leadership, this requires sincerity and discipline. The *I Ching* teaches us,

> Fundamental sincerity is the only proper basis for forming relationships[14].... Thus the sage fosters his character by thoroughness in everything he does. Character is developed by thoroughness that skips nothing but, like water, gradually and steadily fills up all the gaps, and so flows onwards. A certain measure of taking himself in hand, brought about by strict discipline, is a good thing. He who plays with life never amounts to anything.[15]

So, in summary, becoming a modern sage-king or quantum leader requires sincerity, discipline, development of the mind, and lifelong cultivation of the person. The Chinese thinkers believed that it was a goal beyond the reach of most, that very few people ever attain sagehood. But it is an important *aspirational goal*, something that can give our lives and leadership a sense of moral direction. Sometimes the path *is* the goal, just as asking questions can be the answer to life's purpose. We often do our best even in the face of knowing the ends we pursue may never come to be. As Confucius says of the sage in the *Analects*, "Isn't he the one who knows it can't be done, but goes on doing it?" Or, as my grandfather often used to repeat to me as a child, "Reach for the stars, my girl, and then at least you will get to the moon."

Notes

1. See Danah Zohar, *The Quantum Leader*.
2. Richard Wilhelm, *I Ching*, Hexagram 8, *Pi*, Holding Together, Commentary.
3. D.C. Lau, *Mencius*, Book II, Part A, 3.
4. Zhou Dunyi, *Song Yuan xue'an*, 12.1B.
5. Zhang Zai, *Correcting Youthful Arrogance*, Chapter 1, No. 26.
6. *Brihadaranyka*, IV, 4–5.
7. See Zohar, *The Quantum Self*.
8. *The Great Learning*, 1:3, in Gardner, *The Four Books*.
9. Richard Wilhelm, *I Ching*, Commentary on Hexagram 5, *Hsu*, Youthful Folly.
10. *The Great Learning*, 1:4, in Gardner, *The Four Books*.
11. Stephen Angle, *Sagehood*, 9.
12. *The Great Learning*, 1:3, Gardner, *The Four Books*.
13. Richard Wilhelm, *I Ching*, Hexagram 1, *Qian*.
14. Richard Wilhelm, *I Ching*, Hexagram 8, *Pi*, Holding Together.
15. Richard Wilhelm, *I Ching*, Hexagram 4, *Meng*.

6 Twelve Principles of Quantum Leadership

In the Chinese tradition, as we have seen, human beings are fully part of the universe and the natural world, and subject to the same principles of functioning and transformation as the stars and all living things. Indeed, the Chinese argue that, as "the bridge between Heaven and Earth," we humans best play our role in the wider scheme of things when our actions accord with the universal principles of transformation. As the Neo-Confucian thinker Zhang Zai wrote, "One who knows the principles of transformation will skilfully carry forward the undertakings of [Heaven and Earth]."[1]

The leader, especially, is a bridge between Heaven and Earth – knowledgeable about and inspired by the Tao of Heaven and responsible for bringing the same principles that guide the Tao to the way he guides his earthly actions, to the leadership of his organisation; *Tian ren heyi*. In quantum physics, too, of course, human beings are fully part of the universe and nature, indeed co-creators of daily reality in a participative universe where the active human agent and the reality or situation he acts within are always inseparable and co-creative. The quantum leader is guided in leading his company by the same laws of transformation that ensure coherence and constant creativity in the universe, the natural world, and in our living bodies and conscious minds.

We have seen that all living systems in nature, including ourselves, are best understood as living quantum systems, which complexity science calls complex adaptive systems (CADs). And, following the lead of many complexity theorists, Quantum Management Theory argues that human social systems like our companies function best when their leaders themselves, and their leadership practices, are guided by the same transformative principles that allow all other living systems to sustain themselves and evolve. This is very much in keeping with the Neo-Confucian philosophy of Zhang Zai that I have quoted above.

Nature's CADs have 12 defining qualities or characteristics that account for their ability to self-organise and spontaneously adapt both to internal system changes and to the challenges and opportunities of their surrounding environment. In complexity science itself, these defining characteristics are

DOI: 10.4324/9781003623267-9

described technically in terms of biochemical and biophysical processes, but it is possible to express their leadership equivalents in more familiar language as guiding principles for personal and leadership transformation. I offer these now as 12 leadership principles for the quantum leader and recommended in the Chinese tradition as leadership principles for the sage-king.

- Self-Awareness:

    We have seen that self-knowledge, self-cultivation, and constant moral self-improvement are called for in nearly every great text of the Chinese tradition. The *Dao de Ching* tells us:

    Those who know others are knowledgeable;
    Those who know themselves are enlightened.
    Those who conquer others have power;
    Those who conquer themselves are strong.
    Those who know contentment are rich;
    Those who persevere have firm commitments.
    Those who do not lose their place will endure;
    Those who die a natural death are long-lived.
    (Chapter Thirty-Three)

    In his *Inquiry on the Great Learning*, Wang Yangming tells us that to rid ourselves of error and the perils of ignorance, we must constantly reflect on our thoughts and behaviour and "rectify our minds":

    What is meant by cultivating the personal life?.... While the original substance of the mind is originally correct, incorrectness enters when one's thoughts and will are in operation.... He who wishes to cultivate his personal life must first rectify his mind.[2]

    Nature's living systems, CADs, are self-organising. Their sustainability and evolution are guided from within and in dialogue with the external environment. The quantum leader is a self-organising and autonomous person who is responsible for himself and responsible to others, and he wants his company and his employees to be as self-organising and autonomous as possible. To achieve his own capacity to be responsibly self-organising and improve his capacity to serve, he, like the sage-king, must know himself, must know his strengths and weaknesses, must recognise when he is making mistakes, and strive constantly for self-improvement. The unaware person is a puppet of his own lower desires, instincts and negative motivations and is more easily led by "the crowd."

    Quantum leaders do not command and control their employees. Rather, they support and inspire them and guide them with clear operating principles. To achieve this, quantum leaders must themselves have a strong sense of purpose and direction, both for themselves and for the company they are leading. They must know what motivates them and thus what will best motivate those they lead.

All this necessary self-knowledge requires honest, disciplined self-reflection and a firm commitment to self-improvement, and this can only be achieved by a regular practice. In the *Analects*, Confucius' disciple Tseng Tzu describes such a practice,

> Every day I examine myself on three counts: Have I failed to do my best? Have I failed to be trustworthy in what I say? Have I passed on to others anything that I have not tried myself?[3]

Later sages, influenced by Chan Buddhist practice, engaged in meditation. In my own work, I have recommended a reflective practice at the end of each day similar to that of Tseng Tzu but with a wider range of questions meant to explore such things as my interactions with others, things that had pleased or upset me about the day, whether I had achieved something worthwhile that day, etc.

- *Vision and Value Led*:

The quantum universe is directed towards creating ever greater complexity and information. CADs function with the purpose to sustain life and evolve. Because quantum companies are human systems, the purposes, values, aspirations, and motivations of both their leaders and their employees, and a coherent, positively motivated company culture, are a part of their system dynamics. Quantum companies have a clear vision of their purpose, the values that define them as a company, what they want to achieve, and set targets and goals that give a unifying sense of direction to all work activities. All employees know and share this purpose, vision, and values. Each knows his own role and purpose, and how his work is contributing to the larger whole. In the same way, China's philosophers have always argued that a well-ordered and harmonious society rests upon its citizens having a vision of the good human life, and a set of laws, rules, and customs (*li*) to guide them in achieving this. Leaders must provide these.

We have seen that the quantum leader leads his people not with power-over and control, but rather by inspiring them with his own visionary and personal example. And the same idea of the leader runs through all of Chinese philosophy. Confucius says, "Those in higher positions of power are exemplars of those in whose private and public life would exemplify lower positions. When exemplars are virtuous, the people will be virtuous." In the same spirit, the Confucian philosopher Xunzi (298–238 B.C.) focused much of his teaching on government by an enlightened ruler whose private and public life would exemplify *dao*. But how does a Chinese leader become virtuous? Traditional thinkers like Xunzi and Mencius disagree about the original state of human nature. Xunzi believed that human nature is essentially bad, while Mencius argued that man's nature is essentially good. But both agreed that while, in at least a part of our nature, because of our desires, feelings, and sensations, we are tempted towards bad behaviour, having a vision of a good human life, and values cultivated by good daily practices are actually necessary to *be* good. These values are fostered by having a goal to achieve benevolence (*ren*), righteousness (*yi*), and to follow the rules of proper conduct (*li*) that will enable us to achieve these. As Wang Yangming said, "The highest good is the ultimate principle of manifesting character and loving people."[4]

Quantum leaders inspire similar values in their employees by creating a company culture that promotes self-discipline and self-motivation, pride in creating innovative and high-quality products, and self-esteem and reward gained through ensuring good service to customers. In all my own work on Quantum Management, I have argued that inspiring the right motivations in the company culture is essential to higher values being followed.[5,6] While Xunzi argues that a citizen's failure to hold such values is due to his "basic motivational structure," Quantum Management Theory holds that we humans have both negative and positive motivations. True, though studies have shown that 94% of people in most business organisations are motivated by negative energies such as fear, greed, anger, and self-seeking or self-assertion, higher values can be instilled by the positive motivations of exploration, cooperation, self-mastery, creativity, and service. The autonomy and responsibility afforded to employees in a quantum company encourage such motivations.

- *Spontaneous/Adaptive*

Both quantum leadership and Chinese culture stress the importance of spontaneity and having the ability to adapt readily to constantly changing circumstances. In the Chinese tradition, the equivalent of spontaneity is *wu zhi*, from the *Dao de Ching*, meaning "without knowledge," meaning without preconception, without prejudgement. We have seen that today's leaders are acting and making decisions in a dynamic, ever-changing, unpredictable world. Like all living creatures, they must be able to spontaneously adapt as the challenges and opportunities confronting them change. We saw this is why Quantum Management argues companies must be structured in a flexible way that allows for constant, spontaneous adaptation, and why the heavily bureaucratic and tightly controlled organisations of the past must transform themselves into CADs or quantum companies.

In both Chinese thought and quantum physics, spontaneity rules because uncertainty rules. The *Dao* itself is said to unfold spontaneously, as does the constant creativity of the ten thousand things. Quantum physics tells us that when an atomic nucleus emits a decay particle, the trajectory that particle will take or the goal that it will reach are never predetermined. It is the same in the living quantum world, where the adaptations a CAD will make, either internally or in response to the environment, or the mutations it will undergo, are never predetermined or controlled from an outside source. These systems are indeterminate or at least unpredictable. They are poised between order and chaos, between potentiality and actuality, and their indeterminacy makes them flexible, responsive to their environments, and primed to evolve in any direction. This is why quantum companies that function as CADs have flexible, self-managing infrastructures that can respond spontaneously, and thus quickly, to changing customer needs, a changing situation with competitors, or changing environmental or geopolitical situations. The numerous microenterprises called for in Haier's RenDanHeYi Management Model are particularly effective for maximising organisational spontaneity, because they are numerous and independent, and each can deal with changing customer needs or expectations in a unique and creative way. As Sun Tzu advises, "Make war without a standard approach. Water has no consistent shape. If you follow the enemy's shifts and changes, you can always find a way to win."[7] Sun Tzu calls this military strategy "shadowing." In business, it is called being spontaneous and adaptive.

For a quantum company to be spontaneous and adaptive, its leader must have cultivated this skill in himself, and that is why spontaneity is a key principle of quantum leadership. It means making one's tactical decisions in response to the moment, in response to the situation one is confronting "now," not doing something just because it worked in the past, or because it was a step in a preconceived plan or embedded in a particular ideology or doctrine. Confucius warns, "The noble-minded are all-encompassing, not stuck in doctrines. Little people are stuck in doctrines."[8] Spontaneity was also a principle always celebrated in both Chinese traditional art and in traditional thought. Both the traditional painter and the calligrapher let their brush strokes move freely in response to their immediate engagement with the scene they are painting or to the feeling they have when writing.

In the same way, China's sages acted with ease and spontaneity. It was said of Confucius that he "was the sort of man who would hasten his departure or delay it, would remain in a state or take office, all according to circumstances.... Confucius was a sage whose actions were timely."[9] And Wang Yangming speaks of the sage whose mind is not clouded by preconceptions or past actions.

The mind of the sage is like a clear mirror. There is never a trace of an earlier image remaining in the present reflection or a yet-to-be-reflected image already existing there. The study of changing circumstances is something done as the mind reflects on things it encounters.... The mind of the sage responds to each thing as it comes.[10]

This same call to spontaneity runs throughout the Chinese Chan Buddhist tradition.
- *Holistic/Contextual:*
  Both quantum physics and Chinese thought are holistic. That is, both recognise that to understand any situation or to evaluate any decision, one must consider it within the context of an overall pattern or network of

relationships. Everything is connected to everything, and nothing can be intelligently considered in isolation.

The second hexagram of the *I Ching*, *K'un*, The Responding, says, "The sage lets himself be guided; he does not go ahead blindly, but learns from the situation what is demanded of him." In the *Art of War*, too, Sun Tzu advises the strategist to study carefully the situation, or ground, in which his battle will take place:

> The ground determines the distance.
> The distance determines the numbers.
> The numbers determine the calculations.
> The calculations determine your decisions.
> The decisions determine your victory.[11]

Thus, considering the situation means considering the context within which something is being done or is happening, and all the relationships at play within it. The whole of Chinese thought, art, and language operate on this principle. Chinese grammar itself has no verb tenses and no gender dependent pronouns, and a Chinese speaker's words can only be understood by considering the overall context in which they are spoken. A Chinese person will always ask, "What is this matter or problem related to? What are the relationships here?" Confucius says, "In worthy teaching, all things are related."[12] And in both social and business situations, the Chinese always feel that the most important and most trustworthy foundation is to "build the relationship." Zhang Zai tells us,

> The capacity to resonate is a common source amongst the myriad things. It is not an individualistic one possessed by an isolated self. Only the expansive person can make the most of the Way. Therefore, establishment is co-establishment, realization is co-realization, love is always mutual, consummation is never in solitude.[13]

This is very different from Western thought and language, which are expressed in definitive categories of subjects and objects, nouns and verbs, male and female, and past and present, and thus all information required to understand the speaker is contained in one isolated phrase or sentence. A Western person, like a Newtonian scientist, will always want to isolate a situation or problem from surrounding influences and "focus" on what is particular about it. In business deals, they like to spell out in specific detail the individual elements of an arrangement and seal them in a written contract. Even a citizen's rights and responsibilities in a Western society are legitimised in a "social contract."

We saw earlier that quantum physics tells us that reality itself is made of relationships. Indeed, after the quantum vacuum itself, the source of all existing things, quantum field theory teaches that the very first, most primary building blocks of "the ten thousand things" are bosons, particles of relationship. The entire universe is a vast web of relationships in which everything is connected to everything, and thus, to know anything about an elementary particle, a scientist must know what it is in relationship to, in what context he is observing it.

A quantum leader, therefore, always studies the vast network of relationships of which his situation or decisions are a part. If he wants to change a situation or create a better situation for his company, he will change previous or build new relations. And quantum companies like Haier always organise themselves as ecosystems, interconnected and co-creative networks of functions, expertise, and power, and they may want to expand their area of enterprise by including other companies, sometimes even competitors, within a shared, cooperative ecosystem.

- *Field-Independent:*
  Although we are always part of a vast network of relationships and must consider our behaviour and decisions in terms of our relationships to others, we are also the individuals who must make those decisions and have the power to take those actions. Quantum bits are always both wave-like and particle-like, always defined through their relationships and also individual point-sources of action within a network of relationships. As Zhu Xi says in his commentary on *The Great Learning*, "Unlike the luminous virtue (coherence) which is the same in all human beings, each individual has his own luminous virtue (coherence)."[14] So both quantum selves and Chinese would-be sages have a responsibility to cultivate themselves as individuals and to behave with authenticity and integrity in their relationships. They do not just "go along with the crowd," or use the bad behaviour or mistaken thinking of others as an excuse for their own. "The noble minded," says Confucius, "seek within themselves. Little people seek elsewhere."[15]

  The leadership principle of being field-independent means having the ability to stand against the crowd and follow our own convictions. To have the strength and courage to do what we think is right, even if "everyone" is telling us we are wrong. To have the resilience to be unpopular, to not bend if mocked or excluded, and remain true to our principles or vision even when criticised. "The noble minded, says Confucius, stand above the fray with dignity. And when they band together with others, they never lose track of themselves."[16] Field-independent people are also not easily caught up in "popular" ideas, trends of the moment, or the usual way of doing things. They question and think out of the box. Confucius warns, "When everyone hates a person, you should investigate thoroughly. And when everyone loves a person, you should also investigate thoroughly."[17]

  Quantum leaders are pioneers. In giving up traditional power and building companies that allow autonomous employees to work in a self-organising way, they are often making new experiments and taking tremendous risks. They have uncommon visions, and in following them, they risk their careers, their companies, and their reputations. They must be certain in their own minds that what they are doing is right, that it is what *has* to be done. Only the most independent thinkers have this kind of courage.

- *Ask Many Questions:*

Questions play an essential, formative role in the unfolding of quantum processes. Heisenberg's Uncertainty Principle tells us that the questions we ask create the answers that we get. Underlying quantum reality is a vast, deep well of potential, and questions are like buckets we can lower down into this well in order to bring up a bucketful of new reality. In the living world, CADs "ask questions" by continually exploring their environment. Humans are led to ask questions because we are curious, we have a spirit of inquiry, or a passion to learn. Questions also help us get to the bottom of things, to understand how they work, why they happen, or why they have gone wrong. They can take us into the unknown and allow for new discoveries. Reflecting on life's "big questions" can make us wise and make both life and work more meaningful. For Confucius, asking questions was a ritual (*li*) to be observed by the sage, a sign of respect to others, and the way to deal with unusual or awkward situations in a harmonious way. Zhu Xi said of Confucius, "The Master entered the Great Shrine and at every stage he asked questions. Someone said, 'Who says this son of a man of Zhou knows ritual? At every stage, he asks questions.' The Master said, '*That* is the ritual.'"[18]

Too many top business leaders often think they have little to learn, and many discourage subordinates from questioning them or their strategies and decisions. They see being questioned as a lack of respect for their power and position. But Zhang Zai reminds us that, "The great bell never makes a sound itself; it makes a sound only when it is struck. The sage never has wisdom by himself; he possesses wisdom only when he is questioned."[19] Quantum leaders welcome being questioned and make themselves accessible to those who might do so. Some even require their board members or heads of departments to come to them with questions. They would agree with Confucius, who said of an unhelpful follower,

What is meant in saying 'Yan Hui was not one who helped me' is that he had no doubtful questions. If he had doubtful questions, I would resonate with them and through this arrive at interpenetration whether his position was different from mine or in common with mine.[20]

(*Analects*, 43)

In business-as-usual, hierarchical organisations where all power flows from the top, employees are expected to follow orders from superiors and do what they are told. Those who question orders or procedures are considered guilty of insubordination, and often punished. But these are not learning organisations, and they both discourage innovation and deny employee potential. Quantum organisations encourage all to ask questions and value experiments.

- *Reframing*:

Both quantum systems and CADs are constantly restructuring, renewing, and reinventing both themselves and their surrounding environments. This is why they can sustain themselves in ever-changing circumstances and how they can evolve to create new realities or new life forms. Their internal, spontaneous self-organisation has a "felt sense" that responds to the need for this. The equivalent leadership skill that leads to such spontaneous adaptation is the ability to reframe. Reframing requires that we stand back from a situation or problem, and from our own past mental habits and assumptions about how best to deal with these, and view both our own thinking and the situation or problem as though we are a neutral third person, or an outsider coming to them for the first time. We become our own coach or consultant. The standing back needed for reframing requires keen self-awareness, an open mind, and an ability to question ourselves, our own thinking, and the motivations and assumptions that have led to this thinking. We must develop an ability to "let go" of what we have been taking for granted, realising that it is our very own mental habits and the motivations, assumptions, and certainties that have formed them that are trapping us in a "box" that prevents us from seeing things in a fresh and now more effective way. These past mental habits are like the "extremes" warned against by Mencius, who said, "The reason for disliking those who hold to one extreme is that they cripple the Way. One thing is singled out to the neglect of a hundred others."[21]

Reframing also requires the skills of both listening to and seeking the advice of others, and then testing the things they say, even if they are considered experts, against one's own best, most objective judgement. Even experts can be trapped in assumptions of their own, and the most unlikely, most simple employee, can have an important insight or idea. Wang Yangming warned his followers to be alert to this. "In learning," he said,

the important thing is to acquire learning through the exercise of the mind. Even the words of Confucius, if one seeks in one's mind and finds them wrong, they dare not be accepted as true. How much less the words of those inferior to Confucius! If words are examined in the mind and found to be correct, although they have come from the mouth of ordinary people, I dare not regard them as wrong.[22]

Reframing can be even more effective when done in a dialogue situation with ecosystem colleagues and partners, where minds working together from their different vantage points can ask such questions as: "On what assumptions have we been resting our thinking?" "What motivations might have led to the decisions or thinking that created this situation?" "How is the situation or problem we are confronting now different from what we were dealing with before?" "How have others managed such problems?" "What new things could we try?"

- *Celebration of Diversity*:

    Quantum systems constantly throw out a range of feelers towards the future ("virtual transitions") to discover the best way forward. Complex adaptive systems generate mutations as a way of exploring different ways they might evolve. The quantum leader knows there are many possible ways from "A" to "B," many possible strategies, many valuable points of view, many products that might attract a market, each of which is a partial picture of the whole, so he surrounds himself with people who think differently and who hold different points of view. And the sages of ancient China did the same.

    In the *Zhongyong*, the Doctrine of the Mean, we read of the sage-king Shun, "Great indeed is the wisdom of Shun! Shun likes to ask the views of all kinds of people and to investigate the words of those close to him."[23] And we saw just above that Mencius counselled against adhering to just one position or to a single standard. The value of diversity is celebrated in both quantum physics and Chinese thought.

    In the quantum organisation, a diversity of the way to innovate and thus to constantly meet new customer needs is built into the system by the division of multifunctional small teams or microenterprises working independently in a self-organising way to deal closely with customers. Such diversity of approach spreads and enlarges innovation, and also guards against risk, assuring sustainability.

- *Positive Use of Adversity*:

    Wang Yangming wrote, "The ancients have a saying, 'To utilize people's merits is not as good as to utilize their mistakes.' What I have suggested is to utilise their mistakes."[24] He was advising his followers to appreciate the value of mistakes and to make positive use of adversity. This is also a key principle of quantum leadership.

    Living quantum systems, CADs, create order out of chaos. They thrive on mutations, which are genetic mistakes, rejecting the bad ones but moving forward to evolve by using the good ones. Both the quantum universe and quantum biology tell us there cannot be a new creation without destruction. That is why the universe is ruled by two forces, the destructive force of entropy that tears systems apart and the creative drive towards ever-new relationships which lead to new order and new information. The quantum leader not only learns from mistakes but also values them. Thus, he encourages his employees to take risks and do experiments, knowing that these are necessary for innovation. The sage-king, too, finds opportunity in adversity, possibility in defeat. Cheng Yi, a respected teacher and Neo-Confucian moral philosopher who advised the Emperor, was one of the very influential Cheng brothers. He said of the sage, "His mind will not be disturbed by poverty, obstacles, or calamity. He will merely act appropriately.... For sages there are no tragic dilemmas." And Mencius taught, "Incessant falls teach men to reform, and distresses rouse their strength. Life springs from calamity, and death from ease."

But to benefit from setbacks and mistakes as positive gains, the quantum leader must have resilience, or perseverance. He must not give up easily or get discouraged. He must believe in his vision and be able to accept risk and to remain steady in pursuing what he thinks must be done. This kind of necessary perseverance is spoken of in the *I Ching*, which says,

We find ourselves beset by difficulties and hindrances. It is as if someone comes up with a horse and wagon and unhitches them. [But] if a person encounters a hindrance at the beginning of an enterprise, he must not try to force advance but must pause. And take thought. However, nothing should put him off his course; he must persevere and constantly keep the goal in sight.[25]

The ability of an organisation to accept risk and make room for possibly creative mistakes requires that its very sustainability and/or success does not rest upon just one product or process. This, as I have argued before, is why the quantum organisation puts power to experiment in the hands of many teams or microenterprises. If one or two fail or make mistakes, there will be others that deliver successful innovation, and the organisation as a whole will thrive.

- *Humility*:
The director of executive education at a major Western business school criticised 12 principles for quantum leadership for including "humility." She said that business people are not interested in being humble, indeed that a "healthy arrogance" can endow a leader with authority. Many CEO's boast and swagger and feel superior to their employees. Yet in their article on the "Level-5 Leader," the *Harvard Business Review* described humility as one of the two most essential qualities of a transformational leader, "leaders who can transform a good company into a great one."[26] The philosophers of ancient China would agree. Chinese sages were known for their selflessness, despite their many noteworthy qualities. If meeting a man filled with pride about his accomplishments, Confucius would no doubt remind him, "A person may be as nobly endowed as Duke Zhou, but all that isn't enough to inspire admiration if they aren't humble and generous."[27] Wang Yangming echoes this with, "A great defect in life is pride. One must not harbour any egoism in the mind. Being selfless, one is naturally humble. Humility is the foundation of all virtues, while pride is the chief of all vices." And Lao Tzu declared, "He who is great must make humility his base. He who is high must make lowliness his foundation."

There is no place for arrogance among the entangled constituent parts of nature's living systems. No element of a CAD is more "important" than the others. Each is dependent for its healthy functioning on the healthy functioning of all others, each has its strength only because the others are strong. Leading in a self-organising company where important decisions are made by many, the quantum leader is not arrogant or egotistical. He knows that he is part of a larger system and that he must listen to and learn from others, recognising their qualities and achievements and not boasting of his own. He would follow the advice of the *I Ching*, which says,

> It is important to seek out the right assistants, but [the leader] can find them only if he avoids arrogance and associates with his fellows in a spirit of humility. Only then will he attract those with whose help he can combat his difficulties.[28]

Quantum leaders are aware of how much their own achievements are grounded in those of others, and on the gifts of good fortune that life has thrown their way. This, in turn, makes them more sensitive to the needs of others, and they create space and opportunities where their employees can realise their own best talents. Humility makes quantum leaders ask questions and seek assistance, and more ready to admit when they might be wrong and others have better ideas. It leads to a healthy self-criticism and a greater likelihood to do the challenging of one's own assumptions that is necessary for reframing. A humble leader also does not take himself too seriously, and is a bigger person, more at ease with himself as a result. As Confucius says, "The gentleman is at ease without being arrogant; the small man is arrogant without being at ease."[29]

- *Compassion:*

Both the philosophy arising from quantum physics and the works of China's greatest thinkers emphasise the naturalness and the importance of compassion. It is a very necessary quality in the quantum leader. Compassion means "feeling with" and the ability to feel another's suffering or troubles as one's own and care to help them.

Mo Tzu's Zhou Dynasty definition of universal love and mutual aid says, "It is to regard the state of others as one's own, the houses of others as one's own, the persons of others as one's own." [30] Similarly, Confucius said of the benevolent man, "The benevolent man, wishing himself to be established, sees that others are established; wishing himself to be enlarged, he sees that others are enlarged."[31] And in the later Tang Dynasty, Zhang Zai expressed much the same thought when discussing the human capacity to resonate by saying,

> Those who are exhausted, feebled, crippled, or sick, those who have no brothers or children, wives or husbands, are all my brothers or sisters who are in misery and have no one to turn to.... To sustain the heart-mind and cultivate the capacity to resonate is to not be indolent...[32]

Such thoughts appear throughout the whole of the Chinese tradition, and they could not be more quantum.

We have seen that the quantum world is a world of zero distance. There are no borders or boundaries between atoms or their constituent particles, no separation of any kind between them. In quantum physics, as in the reality described by the *Dao de Ching,* everything is connected to, entangled with, everything. Everything is inside everything. An elementary particle's very identity depends upon what it is in relationship to. In the CADs of the living world, all constituent elements or organs of each system are entangled with, defined by, and dependent upon all others. If I want my liver and kidneys to be healthy, my heart must be healthy. If I want my whole body to be healthy, I must eat good food and exercise. In short, I must feel compassion for my body. In the human world, the quantum self is a relational self. I *am* in my relationships. Thus, I am not just my brother's "keeper," I am my brother. If I am to do well, my brother must be doing well.[33] And in a quantum society, no citizen can enjoy the benefits of a well-run society unless all citizens of that society can enjoy a decent quality of life.[34] Compassion for others is a matter of self-preservation.

It is the same in a quantum company. A quantum leader sees his essential role as a servant to his employees. He feels compassion for and cares for them. He provides them with the resources and services they need to do their jobs; he leads in a way that each can fulfil his greatest potential, and he cares that they have good lives. The quantum leader also feels compassion for his customers and for the society in which his company operates, and realises that his own success, the success of his company, the well-being and positive motivation of his employees, the needs and satisfaction of his customers, and the healthy state of his society are all co-dependent, all entangled parts of one larger system. In a quantum company like Haier, compassion is regularly practiced when members of one microenterprise group reach out to help those of another that is having difficulties.

I have described the quantum leader as a sage-king. When Confucius was asked whether he would describe a man who gave extensively to the common people and brought help to the multitude as a benevolent man, Confucius answered, "It is no longer a matter of benevolence with such a man. If you must describe him, 'sage' is perhaps the right word."[35]

- *Sense of Vocation/Purpose:*
"Vocation" comes from the Latin word "*vocare,*" meaning "to be called." A person with a strong sense of vocation feels that his life has an overarching purpose, and he feels called to dedicate himself to serving that purpose. This calling gives his life a sense of direction and will guide all his most important actions and decisions. It is often felt early in life, and a person's sense of whether his life is fulfilling or meaningful will usually depend far more upon his sense that he is answering his "call" than on things like money, personal circumstances, or worldly success. When

very young, the early Neo-Confucian Zhang Zai "felt a sense of mission" to become a sage, and at the age of 15, Wang Yangming declared that he wished to devote his life to achieving sagehood, which he wanted to realise through action. As well as engaging in lifelong self-cultivation, he served society as a general, an administrator, and a teacher. Confucius' strong sense of humility never allowed him to call himself a sage, but he did say, "At fifteen I set my heart on learning."[36]

Chinese people are more likely than many others to have a strong sense of vocation because the Confucian values that inform the culture even to this day stress both the importance of self-cultivation and of service to others, and to society as a whole. Confucian culture places great value on learning and education and on improving oneself so that one can encourage others to do so. Even if people are naturally good, as Mencius argued, they must make great effort all their lives to let this goodness prevail over the temptations of the senses and self-advancement. Thus, *The Great Learning* teaches, "The Way of Great Learning lies in letting one's inborn luminous virtue shine forth, in renewing the people, and in coming to rest in perfect virtue,"[37] and Mencius says,

Heaven, in producing the people, has given to those who first attain understanding the duty of awakening those who are slow to understand; and to those who are first to awaken the duty of awakening those who are slow to awaken.[38]

Chinese. I have found this call to self-cultivation and service to the people particularly strong in my young Chinese students. Indeed, idealism and a wish to serve society is characteristic of many young people in the West today.

In quantum science, a sense of "purpose," or at least of a guiding direction, is found at all levels of existence, both living and non-living. We have seen that the universe itself acts constantly to create new order and information through the formation of ever-new relationships, thus always growing richer and realising more of its potentialities. All CADs, or living organisms, are "called" (function in order) to sustain themselves, reproduce themselves, and to evolve, thus advancing the complexity of life. The Quantum Management equivalent of this drive towards sustainability and growth in the company's sense of higher purpose.

In *The Art of War,* Sun Tzu advises, "Command your people in a way that gives them a higher shared purpose."[39] He also says that "Victory comes when everyone is sharing the same goals."[40] Great, visionary companies that excel at innovation are nearly always founded and/or led by men and women who have a strong sense of vocation about their own leadership, which they impart to the company culture. Such companies know why they exist, what they are *for*, and whom or what they serve. Knowing these things and being dedicated to this clear sense of purpose makes working for it have a sense of integrity and meaning. Their employees are engaged and positively motivated, and thus loyal and productive.

Notes

1 Zhang Zai, "The Western Inscription", *Cheng meng*, Chapter 17.
2 Wang Yangming, *Inquiry on the Great Learning*.
3 *Confucian Analects,* Book 1:4.
4 Wang Yangming, *Inquiry on the Great Learning*.
5 Danah Zohar, *The Quantum Leader*, Chapter 11.
6 Danah Zohar, *Zero Distance*, Chapter 11.
7 Sun Tzu, *The Art of War*, 8:8–11.
8 *Confucian Analects*, I:14.
9 *Confucian Analects*, 2:3.
10 Wang Yangming, *The Instructions*, Sec. 21.
11 Sun Tzu, *The Art of War*, Chapter 4:10–14.
12 *Confucian Analects*, XV:39.
13 Zhang Zai, *Zengmeng*.
14 Zhu Xi, *The Great Learning*, Chapter 1, Commentary.
15 *Confucian Analects*, XV:21.
16 *Confucian Analects*, XV:22.
17 *Confucian Analects*, XV:28.
18 *Confucian Analects*, 3:13.
19 Zhang Zai, *Zengmeng*, 31.
20 *Confucian Analects*, 43.
21 D.C. Lau, *The Mencius*, Book VII, A, 26.
22 Wang Yangming, *The Instruction*, 173.
23 *The Doctrinje of the Mean (Zhongyong)*, 6.
24 Wang Yangming, "Memorial Outlinng Policies for the Frontier," 1499.
25 Richard Wilhelm, *I Ching*, Hexagram 5, *Chun*, Difficulty at the Beginning, Commentary.
26 James C. Collins, "Level-5 Leadership," *Harvard Business Review*, January 2001.
27 *Confucian Analects*, 8:11.
28 Richard Wilhelm, *I Ching*, Hexagram 3, *Zhun*, Beginning, Commentary.
29 *Confucian Analects*, Book XIII:26.
30 *The Works of Mo Tzu*, Book 4, Chapter 14.
31 *Confucian Analects*, VI:30.
32 Zhang Zai, *Zhengmeng*, 62.
33 Danah Zohar, *The Quantum Self*.
34 Danah Zohar, *The Quantum Society*.
35 *Confucian Analects*, VI:30.
36 Confucian *Analects*, II:4.
37 Zhu Xi, *The Great Learning*, Chapter 1.
38 D.C. Lau, *The Mencius*, 5B:1.
39 Sun Tzu, *The Art of War*, 1:14.
40 Sun Tzu, *The Art of War*, 5:4.

Part III
China's Quantum Leaders

7 Zhang Ruimin
Haier's Philosopher CEO

The ancient Chinese were known for using profound philosophy to engage with the world. But this is often true even today in modern China. I have met several Chinese business leaders who have been inspired by Daoism, Chan Buddhism, and/or the Neo-Confucian philosopher Wang Yang Ming to design and run their companies. At business conferences, it is very common to hear speakers quoting from the *I Ching* to make their points. At one company I have visited in Suzhou, Good Ark Electronics, the CEO, Wu Nianbo, motivates his staff and ensures a happy, cohesive company culture that gives people a sense of meaning and purpose about their work, by having all employees read the great classics of Chinese philosophy and Chan Buddhism and regularly discuss them together in study groups – on company time! But I think Zhang Ruimin, the founder and recently retired CEO of Haier, may be unique in drawing both from these philosophies and from their modern expression in quantum physics and complexity science to conceive nearly every detail of the company's management system. It is thus no accident that Haier was the first global company in the world to implement Quantum Management Theory and that Haier's revolutionary RenDanHeYi Management Model is perhaps the benchmark for organisations and institutions wanting to adapt Quantum Management to their own transformation needs, or looking for a Modernised Chinese Management Model to do so.

Zhang Ruimin is called the world's most radical CEO and is known throughout China as "the philosopher CEO." His striking humility, scholarship, bearing, and grace of movement give him more the appearance of a Taoist sage than a business leader. Fitting for a man who says he aspires to leverage traditional Chinese wisdom and philosophy in his management model for today's Internet of Things (IoT) world. Zhang reads at least two or three books every week, and his speeches are always peppered with quotes from great philosophers, both Eastern and Western. Each of his company's internal communications offers a quotation from an ancient Chinese text, like the *I Ching*, the *Tao Te Ching*, or the *Analects of Confucius*, to illustrate his message. Though head of one of the world's leading IoT companies, Zhang famously has no mobile phone or social media accounts, no social circle of friends, and avoids company parties and social activities. He finds such things a waste of time and says, "My time is better spent reading." He has his own very large library in his private office, which is decorated with Chinese traditional art and calligraphic wall hangings bearing quotations from Chan Buddhism and the *Tao Te Ching*.

Like so many boys of his generation, Zhang was forced to leave school in his mid-teens during the Cultural Revolution and sent to work in a rural factory. While there, he had what he told me was the formative experience of his life. "Many of fellow young workers and I," he recounts,

> had ideas for how the factory could be run better and improve its production, but we were always told by our supervisor, 'You are not here to think. Just get to work and do as you are told.' I vowed then that one day I would found a company in which people would be allowed to think.

That was one of his motives for devoting his life to business leadership, but there was another. In a recent conversation, I asked Mr Zhang why a man with his intellect had chosen a business career. "You could," I said, "have been a very distinguished scholar, or even a very senior leader of the Party." (He is currently a member of the Communist Party Congress, and until recently was an Industrial Representative on the Party Central Committee.) His answer spoke directly to the passion for personal autonomy that drives his business philosophy.

"If I had become a professor," he explained, "I would have had to become part of the academic system, and my thinking would have had to conform to academic fashion. And, of course, the Party has its own system, and as a Party leader, I would be expected to follow that. But as a company leader, I could design my *own* system." And, indeed, as the CEO of Haier, he has designed the radically new and pioneering *RenDanHeYi* business model that has won global admiration and acclaim. Recently, after having made several visits to Haier, Chinese Prime Minister Li Keqiang recommended the *RenDanHeYi* model as the business model all Chinese companies should adopt, and many are doing so.

Zhang Ruimin founded Haier 30 years ago by taking over a small and struggling refrigerator company, making very poor-quality goods. One of his first acts as boss was to order the very dramatic "Smashing." In the presence of journalists, he ordered employees to line up 76 of the company's shoddy products and then smash them to pieces with a sledgehammer. "That is the end," he said, "of Haier's association with junk. From now on this company will offer our customers high quality products." But it was not yet the end of hard times.

In the mid-1990s, there was a month when Haier could not meet its payroll. Knowing that would mean his employees, who lived from paycheck to paycheck, could not buy their families' rice, Zhang went to a wealthy landowner in a village near company headquarters in Qingdao to borrow the 10,000 RMB needed to pay his people. However, knowing well that Zhang did not smoke cigarettes or drink alcohol, the landlord decided to play a trick on him. He placed a large bottle of *Baijiu* (a strong Chinese alcoholic drink) on the table at which they sat, and said, I will lend you 1000 RMB for each glass of *baiju* that you drink." The young Haier executive who told me this story continued, "And Mr. Zhang drank the ten glasses of *baiju* and was able to walk away with the 10,000 RMB. He did that for his people, and that is why we love him so much."

Zhang Ruimin's passion for personal autonomy became the central driving principle of all his reforms at Haier: a belief that every employee has unlimited potential and a desire to unleash that potential for the good of both the employee and the company. "In every big company," he says,

> employees are treated like tools to be used by the company. Western companies are dedicated to maximizing share holders' value, not employees' value. I wanted to emancipate these people in accordance with Quantum Management Theory. That is why, from day one when I became leader of this company, I have never stopped thinking about providing opportunities and platforms where everybody can realize their potential. This is the essence of *RenDanHeyi:* putting the value of people at the centre and fully realizing people's potential.

As *RenDanHeYi* evolved over the years at Haier, Zhang's passion for maximising employee potential became the company's defining purpose and distinction as a corporate entity: "Our goal is to offer products that maximize human value by always bringing added value to our users."

Haier's *RenDanHeyi* is a management model created by philosophy and, when properly implemented, always accompanied by a philosophy. This is what gives *RenDanHeyi* its uniqueness, its depth, and its breadth of application. It is philosophy that makes it a new management *paradigm* that can be adapted to the needs of companies other than those involved in retail and to wider fields like education, health care, and even a new model for a quantum global order. Accompanied by philosophy, *RenDanHeyi* becomes a *living* management model capable of infinite adaptation and evolution. Simply taking this philosophical grounding and application for granted, Zhang makes no distinction between Haier, the company, and *RenDanHeyi,* the philosophy. Thus, when giving speeches about Haier, he uses many definitive metaphors that express this link. I want to offer a few of them. In the following chapter, we can then see in detail how these metaphors are embodied in the structure of Haier's unique management model.

Haier Is a Living Fire

Explaining what he believes is the origin of Haier's Ecosystem Brand, and its contribution to the company goal of maximising human value, Zhang quotes from the ancient Greek philosopher Heraclitus, who said, "Fire forms the basic material principle of an orderly universe," and then describes the universe itself as "an ever-living fire." Seeing this as a symbolic way of describing what the quantum worldview says about dynamic relationships as the basis of all existence, Zhang points out that Heraclitus' reference to "fire" connotes the energy of which the universe is made, and the fact that fire moves both independently while at the same time moving everything else along with it. He explains that such an interpretation of the power and nature of fire reminds him of Quantum Management Theory's conception of "the quantum self," an "energy ball" that is both an independent self, devoted to its own self-development, while at the same time being a connected, or relational self that is altruistically devoted to serving others. In Haier organisational terms, the "independent self" is the self-driven and self-organising entrepreneur of a Haier microenterprise, and the "altruistic, relational self" is the individual microenterprise as a member of the ecosystem devoted to maximising human value. Summing up these thoughts, Zhang explains, "This is the philosophical context in which Haier has evolved to become the entrepreneurial ecosystem that it is today, an ecosystem driven by energy, momentum, self-realization, and mutual benefit."

Haier Is the Ocean

Zhang makes much use in his thinking of the Chinese philosophical belief, expressed in Lao Tzu's *Dao de Ching*, that "A person of great virtue is like the flowing water. Water benefits all things and contends not with them." In quoting this, he relates it to two very different conceptions of what a company's purpose should be. Traditional management, he points out, pursues maximum long-term profit and shareholder value, and puts these principles first as the company purpose. But his own belief in designing *RenDanHeyi* is that companies should shift gears and see their purpose as the creation of more value for society. "This quote from the *Dao de Ching*" he explains,

> means that everyone in the company should do their best to serve the world and create value for society, like the nurturing water. All rivers flow into the ocean because this lies downstream and embraces everything. Haier serves the world and firmly believes that there is no one who's unimportant in the world, that everyone is unique and important. So Haier's interests are based on value creation that benefits society and the community.

In this, Haier is also mirroring the view of Quantum Management that there are no "little people," no "unimportant people" in a company, and that all should be given an opportunity to maximise their potential.

Quantum Management argues that a quantum leader is like a Chinese sage-king who leads not with the authority of his top-down power but rather with the authority of his person and character, and that as the leader of a self-organising organisation, he/she should surrender most of a traditional CEO's directive power. Zhang himself further explains Haier's own similar views, its self-organisation and the character of its non-directive leadership, its likeness to the ocean, by adding from the same *Dao de Ching* quote,

> A virtuous person's mind is like the deep water that is calm and peaceful. His heart is kind like water that benefits all. His words are sincere like the constant flow of water. His governing is natural, without desire, which is like the softness of water that penetrates through hard rocks. His work is of talent, like the free flow of water. His movement is of right timing like water that flows smoothly. A virtuous person never forces his way and hence will not make faults.

Haier Is Thought in Action

Zhang greatly admires the philosophy of Wang Yang Ming and has been guided by Wang's stress on "Thought in Action" in his own thinking about *RenDanHeyi*. In a speech he delivered at Harvard University about Haier practice and management insights, he opened by offering a quote from the Confucian *Analects* that had inspired Wang's own presentation of Thought in Action: "The Master said, 'Learning without thought is labour lost; thought without learning is dangerous.'" Zhang went on to explain that Haier's transformation and its leading position as an innovative IoT company owed much to the fact that the company's practice and thinking were constantly informed by extensive reading of both ancient wisdom and modern scientific developments. As I wrote, Zhang is himself an avaricious reader and possesses an almost encyclopaedic knowledge of history and the present, of China and the world at large. Through *RenDanHeyi,* all these thoughts became innovative company action. "Taking in the world's past knowledge as well most advanced IoT theories and thinking," he explained, "we built a robust intellectual reservoir from which we could draw, and that enabled us to experiment with new reforms and constantly adapt to changing times."

Also in citing the philosophical context of Haier's commitment to and resounding success with, innovation, Zhang referred again both to Lao Tzu's metaphor of water and Heraclitus' metaphor of fire, linking the two. Quoting a story in the *Analects* about Confucius that says, "The Master, standing by a stream, said of change, 'It passes on like this, not ceasing day or night,'" Zhang continued,

> In this context of flowing water, we elevated the *RendanHeyi* system's embrace of the ecosystem model so that it ensures both external adaptation and internal company perseverance. We did so with human value maximization as our foundation so that people are granted autonomy while being internally anchored and externally fluid. When such a

balance is accomplished, companies using this model can self-adapt in a fast-changing environment and stay relevant to the times. Organizations and individuals can achieve a state in which they both never forget the origins of their mission, but also attain eternal innovative thinking; they will possess an ever-living fire.

Haier Is the *Dao*

When asked in a conversation with the Deputy Director of China Corporate Culture Institute how Haier has maintained the identity and unity of its corporate culture throughout its development and its transition into a vast ecosystem comprising 4000 microenterprises, Zhang Ruimin quoted what Lao Tzu had said about the *Dao* being the source of all things manifested in the world:

> When *Dao* is in action, one's worldly nature is reversed to the true nature. Gentleness is the way of application of the *Dao*. All things in the world originate from the manifestation of *Dao*, the manifestation of *Dao* is a form of being, which originates from the non-being of the Void, the Great *Dao*.

Zhang takes this to mean that the Dao is circular, working in a gentle and subtle manner. All under heaven (all existing things) are born of tangible materials, which in turn, themselves derive from the intangible. In explaining how the unity of Haier's culture is maintained in a company comprising 4000 autonomous microenterprises, he went on to say that he thought that Haier's corporate culture was like the invisible ocean of potentiality out of which the then tangible, material products produced by the many microenterprises were made manifest. Just as, according to Zhu Xi, the One organising principle of the Void's nothingness becomes "the one principle with many manifestations" of existence, so Haier's culture is the one, unifying, invisible potentiality out of which the many microenterprises and their varied creations emerge.

"By building a culture that fosters entrepreneurship," he explained,

> Haier has cultivated numerous "makers" that create infinite possibilities for future development. As the external market evolves, multidirectional development prompts the many microenterprises to keep abreast of the times through innovation. And at the same time, they are also encouraged to explore unknown territories for future development. It is the intangible corporate culture that has propelled Haier to its leading position in the IoT era.

This *Daoist* explanation by Zhang of how Haier, like the *Dao*, can be one company with many manifestations; its many microenterprises manifesting from the underlying and unifying company culture also illustrates why he has found Haier's *RenDanHeyi* philosophy so akin to quantum philosophy and sees Haier itself as a quantum company. Quantum physics also tells us that all existing things, including ourselves and all the many and varied material things we use and the companies we build, are actualised realities that have emerged from the one vast field of potentiality that is the quantum vacuum. The vacuum itself has no form, but the fertility of its "Nothingness" gives rise to all things that do have form.

Among Zhang Ruimin's favourite books, three are often taught at Haier University, the company's training academy. These are *The Great Learning*, the *Dao de Ching*, and Sun Tzu's *Art of War*. However much times change, and Haier innovation evolves with them, traditional Chinese culture remains the ever-present heart and soul of the company's culture and its *RenDanHeyi* Management Model and is ever relevant. Zhang believes that to run a business, one needs a clear sense of direction. These books, along with knowledge he has drawn from modern science, are the key to the philosophy that has guided his own, and Haier's, sense of direction.

8 Haier's RenDanHeyi Model

The Management Revolution That Emerged from the Philosophy

Haier is the world's largest supplier of domestic appliances and a leading actor in the Internet of Things (IoT) sector, directly employing more than 75,000 people in China alone, and another 27,000 globally, but today the company is better known for its revolutionary *RenDanHeyi* Management Model and its company philosophy than for its appliances. Indeed, because of the almost infinite expansion allowed by that model, Haier has now moved well beyond simply manufacturing appliances into products and services such as clothing, food, wine, agriculture, biotechnology, real estate, and health care, and this expansion is continuing. The company is just now embarking on the manufacture of electric cars.

We have seen that the *RenDanHeyi* model has been built upon the foundations of a powerful company philosophy that has its roots in traditional Chinese wisdom and modern science – quantum physics, thermodynamics, and complexity science. In essence, that philosophy is one of human freedom, human potential, and the creative power of human autonomy. Haier's founder, Zhang Ruimin, believes passionately that every human being has enormous and extraordinary, untapped potential. He has committed his life to creating an organisation that can help individuals realise that potential. "That is what Haier is about," he says, "helping individuals engage their human creative potential in discovering new sources of value for our customers and for each other." This, alone, makes Haier different from almost every company in the world. Most are about maximising profit and shareholder value, and the people who work within them are simply a means to that end. Haier is about maximising human value for all – for the company itself, its employees, its customers, and society at large. The question for Haier was, how do you build an organisation dedicated to maximising human value and human potential and still be a profitable, competitive business that can thrive in the cutthroat world of market capitalism? What is *RenDanHeyi* and how does it work? How has Haier put Chinese philosophy and Quantum Management into practice and become a multinational firm that is a market leader in several major global businesses that are established in regions, cultures, and political economies across the world? We will see that it did so by creating a management model that was so radically different as to seem at first incomprehensible to those familiar with traditional business systems.

Even when first given a personal tour and explanation of Haier and its *RenDanHeyi* way of doing things, most people don't understand what they are seeing. Haier encourages visitors, and at least 10,000 visit every year, but most are puzzled. Even those who now work comfortably and successfully within the Haier system itself. Kevin Nolan, who became CEO of America's General Electric Appliances soon after it became a Haier acquisition, described his experience of first trying to work within the company:

> When I began to work with Haier, I was stunned. I had worked in manufacturing all my life, and yet I could find nothing within Haier that resembled the processes and systems I was used to. I could see that refrigerators and stoves were being made and were leaving factories and getting to customers. But I literally could not understand how it was being accomplished, how it was coordinated.

GEA's parent company, General Electric, was revered for decades as one of the best-managed companies in the world, using traditional hierarchical management processes that see leadership from the top, headed by a powerful CEO, issuing commands down to workers on the shop floor through a complex bureaucratic network of middle managers. Managers manage, and workers do what they are told. But at Haier, there was no hierarchy, no middle managers or bureaucracy. CEO Zhang Ruimin seemed to have no practical leadership function, and numerous small teams of employees seemed to be making decisions and organising themselves. To Nolan, this seemed like chaos unleashed, and yet it was working. How? Why?

The Model

RenDanHeyi (roughly pronounced as "RenDanHoyi") is translated by Haier to mean "the value to the employee is aligned with the value to the user," and this emphasis on an alignment between people who are partners in a win/win relationship is critical to the deeper philosophical roots of the model. A play on the famous Taoist mantra *Tian Ren Heyi*, "Man aligned with Heaven," this emphasises the model's deep commitment to alignments of various kinds, reflecting the Taoist view that when Man is aligned with Heaven, and then brings the power of this alignment to his projects and activities on Earth, such alignment brings maximum benefit and harmony to the whole of humanity. This basic harmonising principle, found in all ancient Chinese philosophies, is the root of a thousand-year-old Chinese preference, still very much alive today, for win/win solutions in matters of both business and diplomacy, something I believe is not properly understood about China in the West today.

RenDanHeyi expresses the very Taoist and quantum insight that we live in a zero-distance world of entanglement, where everything is connected to everything and that no part of a system can thrive unless all parts of the system thrive. In this case, *RenDanHeyi* is saying that the employees (*Ren*) of a company, indeed the company itself, cannot thrive and enjoy value unless the customers/users (*Dan*) it serves thrive and enjoy value from (are aligned with, *Heyi*) their products and services. Having borrowed the term from the writings of Peter Drucker, the *RenDanHeyi* model is also known as the "Zero-Distance Model," as befits any Quantum Management model.

Turning Newtonian/Taylorian Structure on Its Head

Zhang Ruimin says that his motivation to derive a new management model was his strong belief that traditional management theories are no longer relevant today and must be reinvented. Taylorism, and Adam Smith's praise for the division of labour which it incorporates, were designed for the age of the machine, steam engines and internal combustion engines, and the more simple, atomistic, and deterministic, thus predictable, age made wealthy by that kind of technology. Machines are designed by blueprint, consist of simple, separate parts, and operate according to simple, fixed rules, just as companies and other organisations intended to function as no-surprise machines are governed by design from the top and structured according to the iron rules of bureaucracy into siloed functions enabled by workers who will do as they are told, like good machines themselves. But as we have seen, the 21st century is an age of uncertainty, rapid change, and interconnectivity, the age of the Internet and the IoT (everyday objects embedded with devices that enable them to communicate via the Internet), and this new age is enabled by quantum technology and all its associated complexity. Also, today's employees are better skilled and better educated, and have far more potential to offer their companies than serving as mere robots.

Quantum technologies, such as the Internet, like the physics on which they are based, eradicate borders and boundaries with their essential interconnectedness, give rise to unplanned self-organisation on which it thrives, and have infinite potential constantly to generate emergent, unpredictable disruptions. This demands a management model that is itself sufficiently flexible and adaptable to absorb uncertainty and the shocks of constant disruption and to thrive on the opportunities they offer. This is what makes Zhang Ruimin say that, "In the future, all management must be Quantum Management," and why *RenDanHeyi* is an excellent means to implement it.

- *Goodbye to Bureaucracy, Middle Management, and Borders:* Although many business leaders agree with management guru Gary Hamel's saying that bureaucracy "saps initiative, inhibits risk taking, crushes creativity, and is a tax on human achievement,"[1] they maintain it is as a necessary evil for managing large companies and continue to embrace its stranglehold, and the monster is growing. While the number of employees in big companies has increased by only 44% in recent years, the number of middle managers has grown by 100%. Most employees working in companies with a workforce of more than 5000 are buried under eight levels of middle management. They are also assigned to fragmented, siloed functions and expected to follow instructions diligently as these filter down through the hierarchical chain of command. Power comes from the top, and the employees, stifled by all that middle management and its endless rules, regulations, and forms, are treated as mindless robots. The result is not just squandered employee talent and potential, but also employee stress and boredom, low morale, lost man-hours, and, of course, low productivity and growth. Over the past 12–14 years, as we have just noted, the average annual growth in these bureaucratic monstrosities has been only 1.1%, while, by contrast, over that same period of time, Haier's *RenDanHeyi* implementation has delivered 23% annual growth, with increased annual revenue of 18%.

The first rule of *RenDanHeyi* is to get rid of all bureaucracy and clear out the middle managers. Make the organisation lean and agile. The whole idea of linear management goes out the door with this, including all power coming from the top. As we saw, in creating *RenDanHeyi* Zhang Ruimin surrendered most of the traditional powers of a CEO. At Haier itself, today, there are only two layers of management between the CEO and front-line employees. Next, get rid of the siloed, monopolised functions and their borders between employees and replace them with multifunctional, cooperating teams empowered to make decisions, take responsibility, draft strategies, conceive products and/or services, cooperate with each other, and communicate directly with customers/users. After ending the positions of 12,000 middle managers, Haier divided itself into 4000 independent "microenterprises," referred to as MEs. Those now unwanted middle managers were given the choice to join the new model as entrepreneurs running their own MEs, or let Haier help them find jobs elsewhere. While most chose to become *RenDanHeyi* entrepreneurs, others were helped to find employment elsewhere. And countering that original loss of so many jobs, the RenDanHeyi transformation has since created tens of thousands of new jobs.

- *Self-Organised, Self-Motivated, Self-Rewarding*: In quantum systems, any kind of outside influence or intervention "collapses the wave function," i.e. eliminates potentiality. In complex adaptive systems (living quantum systems, including human bodies and human social systems), outside intervention or top-down control destroys the interconnectedness/holism and creativity of the system, eliminating natural evolution (growth) and limiting sustainability. Thus in *RenDanHeyi*, bosses do not assign people to the independent teams, or microenterprises (MEs), do not tell teams what or how to do, do not dictate how teams are composed, or give them fixed goals they must achieve. Instead, the teams are self-organised and self-selecting and work towards more long-term, all-embracing targets.

At Haier, each microenterprise has the "Three Rights" normally kept by senior management in a hierarchical company: (1) the right to set its own strategy, decide its own priorities, how to achieve its targets, and what partnerships it wants to make; (2) the right to hire its own employees, assign them their roles, and decide on cooperative relationships; (3) the right to set the pay rates of each team member and how to distribute bonuses among them. As is the case with sub-atomic particles within the atom, each member of an ME team is able to change their identity (role/function) to stand in for or replace another when challenges or opportunities facing the team system require this. Indeed, even MEs can come and go, as some fail and new opportunities arise.

At Haier itself, which has a company purpose to make everyone an entrepreneur and to give each employee the opportunity to achieve his or her full potential, each of these self-organising microenterprises is a small independent company in its own right, with its own CEO, offering its own products and services, owned by its members, creating and communicating with its own customers, motivated both by a wish to see their company succeed and, thus, to bring value to their customers/users, and rewarded both by a sense of personal achievement and by their ability to keep most of their own company profit and share it among themselves as they choose. Most employees at Haier are paid directly by their customers rather than by receiving salaries from the company.

Again, at Haier, there are three types of MEs/microenterprises: (1) market-facing MEs that deal directly with users wanting the company's range of traditional appliances, though constantly transforming these products in dialogue with changing customer needs and newly available technology; (2) "incubating MEs" that are constantly extending exploring new business opportunities and extending Haier's product and service lines into new areas such as e-gaming, biotechnology, health care, etc., and (3) node MEs that supply component parts, or services like marketing or human resources to the market-facing MEs. Others connect traditional Haier appliance products, like smart refrigerators or smart wine coolers, to other companies offering food or wine products so that these commodities can be delivered to users in a rapid time. These kinds of collaborative activities, and even partnerships based on "temporary contracts" with other companies, have now been hugely extended with Haier's recent move into offering its users "scenarios" and "Eco-System Brands," which I will discuss below.

- *Independent But Aligned:* On the surface, dividing a company or any other organisation into thousands of independent, self-organising entities might sound like a recipe for fragmentation and anarchy. But the *RenDanHeyi* model makes Haier a coherent, well-coordinated organisation that ensures cooperation and alignment between all 4000 of its operating microentities. A strong, central operational system was designed for the entire conglomerate as a first priority. Senior management ensures a company culture that sets common standards and values, common operating procedures and kpi's (key performance indicators) for every ME and its members, and delivers an ever-evolving common strategic direction for the company as a whole. A network of service platforms, each also independent and owned by the platform entrepreneur, and each bringing together more than 50 MEs, acts as a facilitator for coordinating cooperation between the differing MEs, arranging collaborative discussions, and making them aware of joint entrepreneurial opportunities.

Platform owners thus serve the MEs with such facilitation, and also provide the wider service benefits, including startup resources when needed, of a large company to the much smaller MEs, which then function more like startups. They guide and facilitate, but never command. But platform owners are also entrepreneurs in their own right, selling their services to the company's vast internal market, having their own growth targets, and the responsibility of looking for ever more opportunities to create new MEs.

Another level of system coordination is provided by "integration nodes" that exist within each platform. These ensure an integrated supply of component parts from all manufacturing MEs in the company and provide new competence skills to MEs about things such as smart manufacturing and big data marketing information, and administrative services.

These central coordinating structures provide the always necessary, Newtonian "particle aspect" of any quantum organisation, while the self-organising independence of the individual MEs provides the "wave aspect" – thus giving *RenDanHeyi* the dual benefit of any quantum system's both/and, wave/particle duality.

- *The Customer/User Is Now the Boss. RenDanHeyi* insists that the core competency that any organisation must have is the ability to create value for its customers/users. Organisational purpose and success begin and end with a continuing ability to meet ever-evolving user needs. Thus the model requires zero distance between the employees who make, sell, and service products and the users who buy them. "Employees must know their users better than they know themselves," says Zhang Ruimin, and this in turn requires a constant, co-creative dialogue between them via every means available – telephone, Internet surveys and conversations, user feedback mechanisms, face-to-face meetings, and even home visits where relevant. The user should always feel the employee is "at his/her service," contactable, and interested.

    RenDanHeyi assumes that users are partners of the organisation, sometimes even forming new MEs themselves, whose feedback and suggestions inspire new product and service developments, thus stoking the fires of innovation. Some adaptations of the model, employed by Haier itself, allow for users to share the profit or advantages of a suggested new product or service, themselves becoming user-entrepreneurs. This is an implementation of the co-creative quantum relationship between the observer and the observed, which tells us that in observing and questioning reality, *relating to* reality's potential, we make reality "happen," and we turn the possible into the actual. Through observing, discussing, and relating to user needs and suggestions, the employee and the user together co-create innovative realities.

- *Relationships Make the Organisation*: We have seen that our quantum universe, like the universe as described by Daoism, is literally made of relationships, and thus it is relationships that make reality. In quantum physics, there are even "particles of relationship," called *bosons*, described as the "glue" that holds everything together. All four of the Fundamental Forces – gravity, electromagnetism, the strong and weak nuclear forces – are *made* out of bosons, and in a proper understanding of how the universe works, the word "force" itself must really be understood as "the presence of a relationship." And built into the term itself, too, is this understanding of a fundamental, defining relationship between the employee and the management model sees that its fundamental organising principle must be the building of zero-distance relationships.

  In the big e-commerce companies like Amazon and Alibaba, multiple independent companies are serviced by common e-platforms, but there is no relationship between the various companies served, and each has only transactional relationships with its own customers. We have seen that *RenDanHeyi* makes an "up close and personal" relationship between the microenterprises and their users a first priority, but it also mandates cultivating cooperative, zero-distance relationships between all the company's microenterprises. At the very least, there should be shared knowledge throughout the networked system of what others are doing. There must be opportunities for cross microenterprise discussions and a sharing of ideas to cross-fertilise innovation throughout the system. There must be a cultural sense of belonging together for the shared purpose of creating value, for the user, for themselves, for each other, for the company as a whole, and for all the other players in the company's system of relationships – shareholders, the community, the planet, etc.

- *Open Innovation*: Most companies and other organisations are very secretive about their research for innovation. Innovative ideas are seen as company capital, and everything is done to stop possible competitors "stealing" it. But *RenDanHeyi*, which sees the value of all relationships, calls for building a strong, co-creative relationship between company "insiders" and those "outsiders" in the surrounding environment. So Haier, for instance, does not just build zero-distance relationships with its users to mine their needs and thoughts for innovative ideas, but instead goes much further in seeking the creative help of the entire outside community.

  Both known problems facing company R&D, as well as appeals for "bright ideas" about new products or product features, are posted on social media for all to see and respond to. Sometimes, as many as three million people respond to such requests for creative input that relates to a given problem with an existing product or the opportunity to create a new one. The company also communicates regularly with 400,000 "solvers," both individual experts and expert research institutions, as it seeks advice, feedback, and ideas that will further innovation. Those individuals or institutions whose input is used in a successful new product or service are then rewarded with a share in any profit that will be realised. Some even join the company as heads of new MEs.

This "no borders" approach to innovation and creativity means that *RenDanHeyi* sees every citizen as a fellow partner or fellow entrepreneur, thus implementing the quantum and Daoist principle that, because everything in our universe is entangled, because everything and everyone is part of everything and everyone else, there are no "outsiders," there are no "strangers." We are all part of one larger, cooperative, and co-creative system. As Wang Yang Ming expressed this, "The great man regards Heaven, Earth, and the myriad things as one body. He regards the world as one family and the country as one person."[2] Gary Hamel observes that by putting its product development process online and thus open to all, "Haier has reduced the time from concept to market by up to 70%."[3]

- *From Fear to Experiment and Innovation*: Psychological studies have shown that fear is the central motivation driving employees in large, bureaucratic companies and other organisations. A fear of making mistakes. A fear of upsetting the boss. A fear of rocking the boat. Thus, most established companies follow the motto, "If it works, don't fix it." But this makes them essentially conservative and risk-averse, and risk aversion stifles innovation. Our quantum universe as a whole, and the living organisms within it that we call complex adaptive systems, take risks all the time. They thrive on risks because the creative function of risks is built into their nature. Risks are experiments, risks are recce missions into the Future, they are the key to evolution and growth. And being itself a quantum model in practice, *RenDanHeyi* creates a system structure that accepts and thrives on risk.

Each *RenDanHeyi* microentity, because there are so many of them, is free to be an exploratory "finger into the future," behaving like one of the multiple "virtual transitions" that an atomic system throws out in preparation for a move to a different energy state. Each such virtual transition explores one possible path to the future state, and even if this is not ultimately the path the system will take, the virtual transition nonetheless has real effects in the real world as it conducts its trial run. Similarly, each of Haier's many ME projects may or may not succeed in the marketplace. If they do not, they are allowed to fail, without the larger company system suffering any significant consequences. But the failed experiment itself enriches the total system with the experience and knowledge gained through the experiment, and thus was worthwhile. Haier always gains from experimentation, while celebrating diversity and even thriving from any adversity that arises.

- *Ecosystems: A Superposition of Possibilities*. We have seen that the quantum universe is a system of systems. Even each individual quantum wave function is a system of superimposed possibilities, each a rich new reality waiting to happen. And these new realities come about as elements of the system form new relationships. *RenDanHeyi's* employment of ecosystem alliances it this same almost infinite potential to branch out by turning possibilities into new, combined realities in every direction. Many possibilities for many different ecosystem alliances and thus new opportunities are created with each new relationship. This gives a quantum organisation the possibility of constant, endless growth, and even perhaps "eternal life."

  When Haier first introduced RenDanHeyi by dividing the company up into thousands of smaller microenterprises, it found that a kind of dog-eat-dog, zero-sum competition emerged between them. Each thought only of its own possible success. So very soon into the company's transformation, an ecosystem model of win/win cooperation was encouraged. It was quickly noticed that users very seldom came shopping for just one appliance, but rather that someone who purchased a new toaster would soon after, and perhaps simultaneously, order a new microwave and/or a new iron. Similarly, within Haier's own internal market, a market-facing ME needing a component part from one manufacturing ME also needed another from a second, and so on. MEs quickly learned that if they teamed up to form temporary partnerships, they could offer more "total solutions" to users, saving the users searching and shopping time and benefiting themselves from a combined market. Today, Haier is a network of cooperating MEs, sometimes as many as 400 at a time, forming temporary alliances to give users these desired total solutions. As in quantum holism itself, the whole (shared profit derived from the larger market) is greater than the sum of the parts (sold individually, one at a time).

  In 2019, Haier went even further with developing the ecosystem idea by introducing its new Eco-System Brand. Discovering as it went along that users liked buying its own products in combinations that would fill a multiplicity of needs, the company began offering whole "scenarios," such as its "balcony scenario." Originally thinking that people would use their balconies as a place to locate their washing machines, they soon discovered users would like to add a sofa, perhaps a mini sound system, even a piece or two of sporting equipment. The idea for the "balcony scenario" evolved from this, but that required reaching out to other companies, like the sporting goods company Decathylon, with the offer of a temporary contract to supply any such items as part of the new balcony scenario "product," and the whole combination was offered as an Eco-System Brand in which the partnering companies negotiate a temporary contract through which each partner makes some profit from every item included in the scenario package.

With Ecosystem Brands, more borders fell, not just between individual functions and MEs within Haier, but between Haier and other companies. Haier now sees itself more as the "hub" of a vast multi-company network than as a mere "company," and the scenarios/Ecosystem Brand benefit is key to its long-standing preference to aim for growing numbers of loyal customer numbers rather than concentrating on market share as a criterion of success. As Zhang Ruimin summed up this logic, "By fulfilling users every need, we are cultivating lifelong users that will stay with us."

As in the quantum universe, we have seen that with *RenDanHeyi,* everything is connected to everything and the whole system gains from a network of win/win solutions. This gives Haier, as a quantum company, another important feature of quantum physical systems – their property of "emergence," through which an entirely new reality arises from a relationship of constituent parts. We can see how today's Haier has "emerged" out of the relationships within its ecosystem. Indeed, each individual enterprise, through its relationships to the others in *RenDanHeyi,* acquires new, emergent possibilities. Both sustain themselves and grow at the same time. Now functioning like living organisms, they become "living companies." And Haier itself can be described as being like a tropical rain forest – complex, filled with life, dynamic, and having an infinite capacity to grow.

Notes

1 Gary Hamel, "The End of Bureaucracy," *Harvard Business Review*, November–December 2018, 52.
2 Wang Yang Ming, *Inquiry on the Great Learning*, Question 1.
3 Wang Yang Ming, *Inquiry on the Great Learning*, Question 1, 57.

9 Zhu Haibin
Saving the World's Bees

Over the years, I have enjoyed many visits with "The Old Monster of White Horse Lake" in his beautiful garden in the suburbs of Hangzhou. We are always joined by his son and business partner, Zhu Minhao, who translates between my English and the Old Monster's Chinese. We sit by the edge of the lake in the warm sunshine, snacking on Chinese picnics and drinking tea. Sometimes, as evening draws near, we switch our fare to whisky and the Old Monster's Cuban cigars. These days, the garden is filled with bee houses, and our picnics include their honey as well as a refreshing drink of honey, lemon, and passion fruit juice made by his daughter. Local children earn pocket money and test their early entrepreneurial skills by selling this mix to their neighbours and parents.

In the Chinese language, the word for monster means both "bad" and "clever," and it is for this second meaning that the Old Monster has earned his nickname. He has helped many people master entrepreneurial skills and earn money for themselves, and he is a very accomplished entrepreneur himself. His Chinese name is Zhu Haibin, though he prefers to go by his adopted English name, "Eagle" Zhu.

Fifty-eight-year-old Eagle Zhu was born in China's Zhejiang Province in 1965. During China's civil war, his father was a sailor and small boat captain, who later worked as a human resources executive in shipping finance. Eagle studied architecture at Tongji University in Shanghai, and it was there, at age 23, that he first encountered Daoism. He was especially inspired by two teachings from the *Dao te Ching*. One was the statement that "One gives rise to the two, the two gives rise to the three, and the three gives rise to the 10,000 things," and the other was the Daoist stress on the need to serve others. Daoism remains a strong influence in Eagle's life and business practice, both in e-commerce and in his more recent work with bees. Its resonance with much of quantum philosophy was a motivating factor in his later adoption of Quantum Management principles for organising and leading his companies.

Eagle's first business venture was to build a real estate company in Shandong Province, and his management of this, too, was informed by his Daoism. He saw the whole environmental system of which architecture and real estate are a part as something that follows the rule of the universe: Nature following the rule of Heaven and man following the rule of Nature. But by 2008, Eagle was finding the real estate business very difficult, and he felt it was not fulfilling his desire to help people. He wanted to create a company that would enable people to be more self-sufficient and gain better control over their own lives. The result was Wan Se, or W.S., Supplies, an e-commerce company that he established in Hangzhou.

W.S. Supplies acts as a platform that supplies and serves a vast network of housewife entrepreneurs, the "Wan Se Girls," living in China, India, Nepal, and the countries of Southeast Asia. The goods the company supplies are cosmetic items and baby products, and these are purchased in bulk at wholesale prices by women who then organise get-togethers in their neighbourhoods and homes in order to sell them on to family, friends, and neighbours. These women, each of whom is an independent agent acting as an entrepreneur in her own right, reap important financial benefits from their sales activity while at the same time enriching their social lives and enjoying the shared identity of the whole international network. Eagle Zhu himself practices Wu wei leadership, allowing the whole system to self-organise. This has left him free to engage in another business which has really become the passion of his life and the fulfilment of his personal wish to serve both Heaven, Nature, and people – developing the culture and education of the countryside and doing something to save the world's bee population.

Eagle has been fascinated by bees and their habits since early childhood, and as an adult, he became increasingly concerned as bees' habitats and sources of food became threatened. China used to be the world's largest honey-producing country, but this market declined when, like bee farmers internationally, the beekeepers started feeding them sugar in place of their usual diet of natural herbs, and this, too, concerned Eagle. In 2014, he began to experiment with designing digital "smart homes" for bees, complete with software that controls temperature and humidity inside the hive, provides an air conditioning system, monitors the bees' health and activity, tells farmers where they can find the most nutritious herbs in their area to feed the bees, and is equipped with an alarm to ward off bears. More recently, he has been developing software that will allow bee farmers to gather their honey more safely. By 2018, the technology and software were sufficiently developed that the new Wan Se Bee Park ("Colorful Bee Park") and Research Center could start operating as a commercial business. Today, Eagle is joined and aided by one hundred colleagues and advisors, many of them government scientists and economists, and the whole project has the backing and support of the Chinese government, which sees it as helping to rejuvenate China's rural districts.

A traditional beehive can produce at most 5 kg of honey in a year, but each Wan Se smart beehive can produce ten or more kilograms, and the bees themselves live longer. A bee farmer can tend to at most 30–50 traditional hives, but is able to manage 100 of the digital hives, thus at least quadrupling his income from his annual honey crop. Wan Se also encourages the farmers using the hives it provides to feed their bees on natural herbs rather than sugar, further ensuring both production and quality of the honey they make. Insurance companies are willing to back these practices up with certificates guaranteeing the health and living conditions of the bees, providing farmers with a further marketing tool.

Since the company's founding, Wan Se Bee Park has produced 20,000 smart beehives. Ten thousand of these are being used in 18 bee farming villages all across China, and 10,000 have been distributed internationally. Eagle Zhu's vision is the eventual production by medium-sized companies of one billion smart hives, distributed internationally. If just 100 million of these are kept in China, it would create a total of 20 million associated job opportunities in the rural countryside. To assist with the growth of this industry, the government is creating more education programmes and scholarships for young people to study the art of beekeeping. At its own headquarters in Hangzhou, Wan Se offers bee education programmes for school children.

At the Wan Se Research Institute, scientists are developing new products that can be produced from honey, including cosmetics, nutritious foods, and medicine. Some of the Chinese herbal medicines being made from the honey can help the deaf and blind regain some of their faculties. Through his W.S. Supplies e-commerce company, Eagle Zhu distributes these products to his international sales network of "Wan Se Girls," adding to the products from which they can derive income.

Wan Se Bee Park adopted and works collaboratively with the once very poor rural village of Linpu, located on the outskirts of Hangzhou. The company has provided 100 bee farmers in the village with 100 free digital hives each and instructed the farmers how to use the software. It also purchases and markets the honey produced at the village. Eagle's son, Zhu Minhao, took me on a personal visit to Linpu, and I witnessed the great improvement the wealth and industry from the new digital bee houses have brought to the village. Now, a government-designated "model village," Linpu, has leafy, tree-lined paved roads running through the village. A smart new central community hall provides meeting rooms, a restaurant and a tea house where residents can relax and socialise, and a large exhibition hall where the many products made from the village's honey and tea crops are displayed and sold. Village residents' homes were all renewed and upgraded as part of China's antipoverty campaign. A proud young bee farmer who had earned a PhD in bee science walked me through the village fruit orchards and tea fields to a collection of the hives that he keeps and demonstrated how he gathers the honey. Remarkably, he wore no protection, telling me that Chinese bees are less aggressive than other bee varieties. They are also able to fly to higher altitudes than most other bee species, thus able to access the wider variety of nutritious herbs that grow in high mountain regions.

The Wan Se Golden Bee project and its affiliated research centre have given Eagle Zhu the opportunity he long sought to establish a company following the Daoist vision that our enterprises here on Earth should follow the rule of Heaven (the way of the cosmos and nature). It has also enabled him to put both Daoist and Quantum Management *wuwei*, or hands-off, leadership into practice. Once he has supplied the beekeepers with their smart hives and taught them how to use them, he exercises no management control and no production pressure. Each beekeeper is a self-organising entrepreneur in his own right, raising his bees and harvesting their honey without interference, and keeping all profits he earns from selling his honey. Helping to improve the farmers' lot still further, the Chinese government issues e-money that combats corruption, and the technology provided by the Wan Se Research Center helps them know how to use this e-money to increase their income and improve their tools through online systems.

Eagle Zhu is a quantum leader par excellence. Idealistic, inspired and inspiring, he has devoted his business life to service – service to nature, service to the many independent entrepreneurs he has enabled, service to a better life for people living in isolated or rural districts, service to the consumers who have access to more healthy and high-quality produce and, ultimately, service to society and the universe. His entrepreneurial activities have created many jobs, and they have enabled people to develop their own potential to earn a better income. When he retires, he wants to become a bee farmer himself.

10 Li Ling
Quantum Management for Schools

So far, I have been writing about quantum leaders mainly as business leaders, and Quantum Management as a new way of structuring and leading companies. But on my most recent visit to China, I learned that Quantum Management is being used as a new way to organise schools and to provide new thinking about how to reform and modernise education. Group project-based learning is replacing the more passive classroom learning, children are being asked to relate their school work to daily challenges in their lives and the world they will encounter beyond school, pupils are being offered autonomous choice about how and what they learn, becoming more responsible for the daily running of their schools, and the concept "everyone is a leader" is being applied to pupils as well as teachers. *Wu wei*, or "don't interfere," is becoming a principle practised by headteachers and school boards.

Few of us who have endured the seemingly endless years of school-as-usual would doubt that both education and the daily school experience are in serious need of reform and modernisation. In a 2023 Gallup poll of students in all of America's high schools, students rated their schools at C+ on the three qualities of preparing them for the future, making learning exciting, and meeting their special learning needs. Ten per cent of students rated their schools at D or F.

The world children must enter as young adults today is unrecognisable from the world that education was designed to serve at the end of the 19th century, when general education for all was introduced. The world of the 21st century is one of dizzying, fast-paced change, questions, and uncertainty, requiring that school graduates can think independently, critically, and creatively. Technology has radically altered the challenges and opportunities we face in life and the skills we need for work. An ability to work with digital technology and to get the best advantages from AI systems is becoming almost mandatory in the workplace. The leadership crisis we see in business is mirrored by a general crisis of authority and respect in society at large, and students as well as workers are demanding more autonomy and decision-making power. We face many problems today that we feel ill-equipped to solve, and it often feels there is no one in charge, no one "out there" who is better equipped than we are to solve them. Some of us even begin to doubt that human beings, as we are, have the *capacity* to solve the problems we ourselves have created. Indeed, humanity may be at an existential turning point where we either make a quantum leap forward in our intelligence and wisdom, perhaps in our very nature, or we perish. And yet the schools meant to prepare us for life remain largely unchanged, seemingly unaware they have become outdated and irrelevant.

I hated school as a child, having to sit still at a desk all day, not really understanding why I was forced to be there. My greatest problem during my lessons was struggling to stay awake. I often pretended to be ill in the morning so I could stay home, or I hoped that a big snowstorm would close the schools. During the Cold War in the 1950s, I used to wish the Russians would drop an atomic bomb on my school. I learned far more on my own at home, where I could read and do projects that interested me, and do so without waiting for others to "catch up."

For the first two years of my school-age life, I was home-schooled by my grandmother, who returned home each day from her own teaching job at the local country school and sat with me to improve my reading and maths skills. During the day, while my friends sat in school, I read books that interested me, attended to my vegetable garden in our backyard, and built projects with my free play time. After watching a television programme about "Tom Corbett, Space Cadet," I built my own rocket ship out of orange crates and spare pieces of wood, though I did get into trouble when I visited the local gas station to buy fuel needed to get to the moon! I collected and dissected grasshoppers and worms, and watched the busy lives and nest building of the ant colonies in the garden. I established an Astronomy Club in one of my grandmother's chicken houses and covered the walls with pictures of the planets and star navigation charts. I spent hours flying my kite, advised about air currents by my grandfather, who had learned how best to use water currents to pilot his boat when a tug boat captain on the Great Lakes. My grandfather was the town's Justice of the Peace and held court each afternoon in our living room. I was allowed to sit in on his court sessions and hear the problems and quarrels that brought the troubled adults there. Each day was a learning adventure, with free play, listening, doing, and observation as my learning tools. But then, at age 8, I moved back to the city to live with my mother and was enrolled in regular school. The learning adventures were replaced with sitting still and rote memorisation for eight hours every day, and the joy of free play was replaced with fear of my often very strict teachers and their threats of punishment. The homework assignments I was forced to do were dull and repetitive.

I had so many questions as a child, but these were seldom explored in school. Indeed, the teachers often scolded me for asking questions, told me just "to be quiet and listen to what I am telling you." In high school, my physics teacher used to rush into the men's room whenever he saw me approaching in the hall. My mother, a fellow teacher, asked him why he did this, and he said, "I'm afraid she is going to ask me a question." Indeed, I might have wanted to ask him about quantum physics, which I had discovered and learned about in my free time at the age of 15. This teacher didn't want to hear about or share the atomic projects I was building in my bedroom at home – an electron accelerator and a Wilson cloud chamber for tracking the movements and collisions of subatomic particles. He was just afraid of my questions.

And yet, questions are the source of all exploration and creativity, the signs of a child's natural curiosity and hunger to learn. We have seen that quantum physics has shown that questions and experiments are the very source of reality creation itself, those buckets we drop into the sea of infinite quantum potentiality to draw up new buckets full of existing actuality. It is also with our questions that we creatively discover ourselves, with which we tie the fragments of our experience together into a meaningful whole, into a meaningful life. To smother all that with a schooling regime that discourages asking questions is child abuse.

In sharp contrast to this dull and torturous experience that is education-as-usual, could we imagine education that is an exciting adventure of mind-expanding discovery? Education that is led by a child's natural curiosity and his/her endless questioning? By the child's natural desire to learn? Can we imagine teachers who learn *with* their students, and who thrill when their students' knowledge surpasses their own?

When I visited the Dayawa Beijing Normal University Experimental School in Huizhou, a city in southern, Guangdong China, I discovered the kind of school and the kind of adventurous learning experiences that would have provided this kind of exciting education, the kind of school that I had longed for during my own tedious school years. The children at this primary school were happy, smiling, and lively, rushing up to greet me and eager to show me their projects. The teachers were friendly and informal, and shepherded the children about and shared in their enthusiasm as though they were their proud older brothers or sisters, gently guiding them without the usual strict, disciplinary control. Finding it unusual to meet a foreigner, both children and teachers showered me with questions and curiosity. The atmosphere of this school, the first in China, and perhaps the first in the world, to use Quantum Management principles for school governance, was joyful and stimulating, its new buildings and their campus beautiful, and the bright classrooms were filled with projects, all the walls covered with children's artwork and mottos about self-improvement – never feeling defeated, helping others, and the thrill of learning. Let me introduce you to the remarkable headmistress of Dayawa Experimental School and to the revolutionary educational and governing practices she has put in place.

Fifty-one-year-old Li Ling is both the Headmistress of the Dayawan Beijing Normal University Experimental School in Huizhou and a Professor at Beijing Normal University. She is also most definitely a quantum leader – wise, caring, learned, friendly, and very professional; an excellent role model for her students and teaching staff. Huizhou is just across the bay from Hong

Kong. The Dayawan Experimental School was established in July 2016 as a pioneering institution in China's drive towards educational modernisation. Li Ling is the Communist Party Secretary of her school and an adviser to many other schools. Every year, she receives thousands of education colleagues at her school in Huizhou. During her long career as a teacher and then a headmistress, she has attracted much recognition and won many awards: National Education Award as national outstanding teacher, National Outstanding Principal, and Top Ten Innovative Education Leaders in Shandong Province.

Li Ling was born and grew up in China's more northern Shandong Province. Her grandfather practised Traditional Chinese Medicine, her father was a teacher, and her mother was a housewife. She has one daughter, who is a headmistress in Toronto, Canada. Li Ling was raised surrounded by teachers, and knew since early childhood that she wanted to be one when she grew up. But her own teachers were not always a positive experience. She remembers being often afraid of them because they were stern and seldom smiled. She promised herself that when she became a teacher herself, she would always smile. In fact, as a child, Li Ling was so well known for her own happy smile that her family gave her the pet name, "Xiao," the Chinese word for "smile." And throughout her long teaching career, she has been known as "the smiling teacher."

Indeed, smiling became a principle and a focus for Li Ling as both a person and a teacher. The meaning of the word became her inner drive, and she came to believe that smiling can overcome any difficulties and solve any problems. Throughout her life, she has used smiling as a form of personal meditation to break through her own problems, limitations, and issues. She encourages smiling as a keystone of school culture, and instructs both students and teachers, "Let saying "Ni hao! (Chinese word for "Hello") become your daily habit." This is because when you say, "Ni hao," your face always breaks into a smile. On the day I visited Dayawa School, everyone did greet me with "Ni hao!",", and I saw many very happy smiles.

After several years as a young teacher of maths and the Mandarin language, Li Ling was appointed Principal of Beishi Qingfu Qingdao Affiliated School of Beijing Normal University, a school with 4000 students on three campuses. This appointment was the fulfilment of another meaning for her childhood pet name "Xiao." As well as "smile," xiao also means "principal." In almost no time, she had raised this school from a poor, failing school to one of the best in the province, and she gained a reputation for her unique approach to governing a school. Li Ling had always believed in child-centred learning, with a prime goal of making school a happy experience for children. At this Shandong school, she introduced many early experiments in giving children more control of their own learning experience, teachers more freedom to choose how and what they wanted to teach, and parents more involvement in the daily life of the school. Having become known for this more advanced educational philosophy and unique style of school governance, she was eventually asked by Beijing Normal University to lead an even more bold experiment in school modernisation at a new school in Huizhou.

The Dayawa Experimental School was opened for the first time in July 2016. For several months prior to this, new teachers hired by Li Ling held community events and workshops to inform local parents about the new school's more child-centred approach, telling them that meeting students' needs and making school a happy experience would be the highest priority. During May and June, Li Ling herself gave several community presentations to describe the new school's philosophy and approach. The school, she said, would empower children's own initiative and self-motivated, self-organising powers. It would work with their inner drive and emphasise good character that would help them become better citizens who could contribute more to society. Most of all, the learning environment would be positive and happy, and there would be zero distance between the school, parents, and the community. Still, on the first day of the school's opening, she and the staff had no idea how many students would be brought there for enrolment – 10 or 12? A few dozen? But in fact, 432 students turned up with their eager parents. Today, the school has 2000 students.

Li Ling immediately introduced a decentralised, Quantum Management approach to governing the school. She surrendered her traditional principal's control and powers, and declared that everyone would be a leader – teachers, parents, and the students themselves. This new system required that a great deal of trust would be placed in both teachers and children at the school. Such trust is an essential characteristic of Quantum Management. Daily learning is project-based and hands-on, creating a "makers' culture," with children working in small teams and, with the help of their parents and teachers, initiating their own projects. At the beginning of each school year, children and their parents are presented with an array of learning possibilities and programmes, from which they choose, and then both pupils and teachers write a "vision statement" about what they want to learn or teach during that year. If, by the middle of the academic year, these feel unsuitable or the children's interests change, they can switch to a new programme for the duration of the year. The most important thing considered is having the children contribute their own interests and enthusiasm to learn. These practices enable the self-motivation and self-organisation called for by Quantum Management. Teachers, too, can choose at the beginning of each school year what subjects they would like to teach, or whether they would like to teach that year at all. They are each given three options about what they want to do and teach during that year, and what other teachers they want to work with. A Group Leader chooses his or her team, but joining the team is then voluntary for each individual. Also, at the beginning of each year, every teacher has to "sell" him or herself to both parents and pupils. Every teacher has a common goal during the year to make every student happy and filled with excitement, and successful at achieving required academic knowledge, but each is free to approach this in his/her chosen way.

Every step is taken to make the learning experience holistic, "entangled," everything connected to everything, with the school practising a "flowing soul" philosophy – making certain everything is in a state of flow, flowing together, and that this is getting into the children's souls. This enables the children to gain a sense of why they are learning these things. Every week, there is a synchronisation meeting involving all members of the school community, including parents. People-to-people relationships are stressed, and children are encouraged to be kind, friendly, and helpful to each other. Teachers and teaching teams cooperate with each other, and dialogue between teachers is constant. All learning materials are integrated, so that children gain a good understanding of how the different subjects they are being taught relate to each other and relate to their lives in their families and community. Education goals are always chosen organically to meet the interests of the state, parents, teachers, and pupils. Both children and teachers grow the vegetables and flowers in the school garden, and children grow a rice crop each year. Wanting them to learn early to take responsibility for their own lives and wider society, children are given the job of cleaning the school themselves, including washing the windows.

Parents are encouraged to be an active part of the school's daily life, attending their children's presentations, and once each year, contributing a personal learning presentation of their own. Additionally, every week, some child's mother comes to the school to offer a presentation or read a book. This is called "Story Mother." Eighty per cent of the school cooks and dining staff are parents. This parental involvement creates a natural connection between children's school experience and their lives at home. At the beginning of each school semester, parents and teachers are also given a suggestion of one book to read in common and then discuss together in small groups. This year, when I visited, the book everyone was reading was *Who Moved My Cheese?* And at the end of each semester, there is a group discussion and related activities for everyone who has agreed to read the book. This may involve video, pictures, acting, etc. Thus, parents share in the learning experience offered by the school. Each Friday afternoon finishes with a "Chaos Session" involving both pupils and parents, 90–120 minutes of free exploration together with no boundaries. Finally, at the beginning of each school year, and continuing throughout the year, different discussions are held that integrate the views of the local school board, directors of education, the parents, teachers, and students. This ensures constant, dynamic interchange of views, reassessment, and future planning.

At the end of each semester, there is an assessment of student progress, with a large emphasis placed on a "fuzzy assessment" that will not restrict either learning or teaching. The children are rated on their overall academic performance, and each takes the Stanford Performance-based Assessment, but overall progress is judged by children's exhibitions about what they have learned that year, and by a teacher's personal observation assessment. It is realised that different children learn at different rates and have different talents, so each is rated as an individual according to his own effort and potential. Children are rated largely on the three criteria: sense of belonging, happiness, and a flowing soul.

Extra-curricular activities are emphasised at Dayawa School, and 60% of students stay after school for 90 minutes each day to participate in these. The school is especially proud of its physical education programme and achievements, with all pupils getting 100% on national tests for physical education standards, and students winning many awards in national competitions. But the benefit gained from attending this school goes far beyond just physical prowess. Graduates of the school also do better on academic tests than those from other schools, in later years achieving higher marks on the national, middle school *zhong kao* exam, and then on the very demanding *gao kao* exam that all Chinese students must take at the end of their high school education.

Li Ling's inspiration for her revolutionary teaching philosophy had many roots. Her grandfather's practice of Traditional Chinese Medicine grounded her during childhood in the principles and mindset of traditional Chinese philosophy, though she says she was unaware how very Chinese her thinking is until many years later, when serving as a visiting professor at Brock University in Canada's Toronto area, a fellow professor frequently commented on "how holistic" her thinking was, how different from Western thinking. She had also been very inspired by reading the philosophy of Kazuo Inamori, the founder of Japan Airlines, who wrote the books *A Compass to Fulfillment* and *Respect the Divine and Love People*. Another fellow professor at Brock University had advised her to read complexity theory, and two professors from Beijing Normal University often spoke about connectionism, the advantages of networked as opposed to linear thinking, and the vital importance of asking "Why?" But then, in 2019, she read my book, *The Quantum Leader*, and discovered Haier's *Rendanheyi* management model, and she realised that Quantum Management was what she had been instinctively practising all along, that it provided the total framework and basis for everything she was trying to achieve. Thus, she began to describe her own work as "Quantum Management for School Governance." After reading my book *Zero Distance* in 2021, she refined her own practice of Quantum Management for schools still further.

All this new philosophy and new practice at the Dayawan School has been so successful that in spring 2023, the education authorities for the whole of Guangdong Province and China's Bay Area announced that Quantum Management would be adopted for all schools as the means for modernising Chinese education. Ninety-three million students attend the schools that will be involved. And China's National Innovation Center (NICE), a huge scientific and technological development conglomerate of one hundred universities and over 300 business enterprises, is now hoping to use Quantum Management in their own efforts to reform Chinese higher education. To make more clear to readers just what these movements are putting into place, I will summarise here the defining principles of Quantum Management for education, and the way these reflect Chinese traditional thought:

- *Self-Organising:* The ancient Chinese always believed the *Tao* is self-organising. Lao Tzu's principle of *wu wei* tells us not to interfere with this, not to try to control it, but rather, "to go with the flow." Living quantum systems, CADs, are self-organising systems, functioning and evolving according to their own organic, inner system logic. Any outside or top-down control destroys sustainability and evolution. Quantum schools operate as self-organising systems, free from heavy top-down control and bureaucratic directives. They ensure maximum autonomy for all teachers and students to make decisions, take creative initiatives, interact with each other, and achieve their own best potential, guided by common purposes and goals, and their own inner drive. Children are self-motivated because learning is fun, and school is a happy place. Knowing they own and are responsible for their studies and teaching, both students and teachers are more highly motivated, committed, and productive. Quantum school principals lead, not with power, but with the moral authority of their character and personal example. They inspire and facilitate rather than control. This self-organisation requires a high level of trust in both students and teachers.
- *Holistic:* All traditional Chinese thought teaches that everything is connected to everything, everything inside and a part of everything. Quantum living systems, CADs, are holistic – everything is connected to everything, and the behaviour and identity of every element are defined by its relation to the others and to the system as a whole. There is no separation. There are no boundaries within the system or between the system and its environment. Quantum schools provide an "entangled," well-integrated system of learning, where everything is connected to everything. Students and teachers work in self-organising, multi-dimensional project teams where the learning objectives of all subjects are closely interrelated. These teacher/student project teams learn in close, co-creative relationships with other teams, with parents, school authorities, and the community. Parents are encouraged to be involved with, and actively participate in, the daily life of the school. There is constant communication, cooperation, dialogue, and reassessment involving all members of the school ecosystem – students, teachers, the principal, parents, and educational authorities.
- *Celebrate Diversity:* China's ancient thinkers celebrated diversity in unity: "one principle with many manifestations." Quantum systems are superpositions of multiple potentialities, and as they evolve, they send out multiple "feelers into the future," simultaneously exploring many ways forward. Nature and the process of evolution thrive on diversity. Quantum schools

celebrate the diverse abilities, potentials, learning styles, and interests of all students, the diverse skills and interests of teachers, and the diverse, infinite potential of things to be learned. They are committed to "letting a thousand flowers bloom."

- *Experiment! Ask Questions:* Confucius asked many questions! In quantum physics, questions (and experiments) creatively discover answers. Quantum schools encourage students to ask questions, to explore with their questions, and to love the questions. Teaching is question-led.
- *Build Relationships:* Chinese culture cherishes relationships. It teaches that we *are* our relationships. The quantum universe is literally made of relationships. New relationships create new realities, and all things and events exist within, and are affected and defined by, the web of relationships of which they are a part. Quantum schools foster good, caring, and compassionate relationships between students, between students and teachers, and between the school, parents, and the community. School ethos and activities create opportunities for co-creative, cooperative relationships to thrive.
- *Take Responsibility:* Lao Tzu said, "I am the world, I am responsible for the world." Confucian thought teaches that we are responsible for the well-being of others and the good of society. Quantum thought says we create the world; therefore, we are responsible for the world. Quantum schools give children responsibility for their learning and for each other, teachers responsibility for their teaching and the well-being of colleagues. Good character and good citizenship are emphasised. Children practice this good citizenship and responsibility in all daily school activities and by cleaning and caring for the school themselves. Children and teachers are trusted.
- *Joy:* Quantum schools are joyous, happy places, where learning and good fellowship are fun.

11 Liu Qing

Towards China's Knowledge & Innovation Economy

Fifty-eight-year-old Professor Liu Qing is the President of NICE, the National Innovation Center par Excellence, a vast education, research and technology development network located in the Yangzte River Valley, and a member of the National People's Congress, China's parliament. He is a quintessentially "nice person," with warm brown eyes that are always smiling, a quantum leader and sage-king who is sensitive, patient, and alertly attentive to whomever he is dealing with. Despite his long working days and a frenetic schedule that takes him all over China and requires frequent trips abroad, he is a remarkably calm personality who radiates serenity. And despite his many achievements as a research scientist and entrepreneur, and his very prominent position in society, he is a strikingly humble man. He may owe these personal qualities and his high ideals about wanting to serve society to the great influence of his grandparents and their wisdom drawn from the *I Ching*.

Liu Ching's grandfather was a local *I Ching* master who was devoted to serving his neighbours, using *I Ching feng shui* principles to help village people plan and build their homes. He was also a very serene person, afraid of nothing. Liu Ching remembers that as a boy, he was frightened of lightning, but his grandfather told him that only people who mistreat their parents and elders should fear lightning. The lesson he drew from this was that, if you are good in your heart, you have nothing to fear.

Born in the southern city of Chongqing, Liu Qing was a precocious boy who received his undergraduate degree from the University of Chongqing at the very young age of 15. He then went to the far northern city of Harbin to do his master's and PhD research in materials science. He married his doctoral professor's daughter, his beloved wife Yao Yeh, who is also a successful social enterprise entrepreneur and a devoted Buddhist, and the young couple moved to Beijing, where Liu Qing did post-doctoral research in Science & Technology at Peking University.

After completing his research at Peking University, Liu Qing moved on to Denmark, doing research in materials science for seven years at the Danish National Academy of Science Riso Laboratory. He returned to China in 2000 to take up an appointment as Professor of Materials Science at Tsinghua University in Beijing. Still only 36 years old, he was the university's youngest ever professor. With a Danish colleague, he received a government grant of 12 million RMB to conduct research in superconductivity, but the terms of the grant required that they must use the whole sum within just one year. There were so many government restrictions on how the grant money could be used that the pair had difficulty finding ways to use it all. This left him with a lifelong distaste for bureaucratic restrictions and regulations, which he feels interfere with the efficient running of companies. So he decided to start his own company developing technological applications of superconductivity, the first of many companies he has established over the years. But at that time, he knew nothing about organising and running a company, so he had to start by purchasing a book, *How to Write a Business Plan*! Liu Qing's tech company was the first ever company founded by a Tsinghua professor, and he and his Danish colleague were invited to demonstrate their superconductivity research, their company and its products, to Chinese President Jiang Jeh Min as part of the celebrations to mark Tsinghua's 90th Anniversary in 2001. Tsinghua proudly claimed the credit!

After four years as both a professor and an entrepreneur at Tsinghua University, Liu Qing took his research and business activities back to Chongqing. In 2007, he was appointed as the Dean of the School of Science at Chongqing University, and then he became the university's Vice President in 2011. In 2021, he was recalled to Shanghai by the then Mayor of Shanghai, Li Qiang, now the Premier of China. Li Qiang wanted to found NICE as a big umbrella organisation to oversee, further develop, and expand the many research, tech development, and engineering educational reform activities of JITRI, the Jiangsu Industrial Technology Research Institute. JITRI was founded in 2013, and NICE began operations in June 2021. In looking for someone to fill the new presidency of NICE, Li Qiang was looking for someone with scientific, academic, management, and entrepreneurial experience who had also had experience abroad. Liu Qing handsomely met all those qualifications, the only one able to do so.

Liu Qing was also well known to the Vice Governor of the Ministry of Science and Technology through their joint membership of the High Tech Expert Committee on Advanced Materials. As a member of that committee, Liu Qing had suggested a Third Reform to President Deng Xiao Ping's "Great Reform and Opening Up" initiative, begun when he became China's leader after the death of Mao. Deng Xiao Ping's Two Reforms were to allow farmers to own their own land, and to allow the formation and activities of private industry. The Third Reform suggested by Liu Qing was for China to become a Knowledge Economy and an Innovation Economy, and he pointed to JITRI as a founding example of the kind of organisation that could help the nation build this. As a result, in 2018, on the 40th Anniversary of China's Reform & Opening Up, JITRI won an award from Jiangsu Province for achievements that had contributed to Reform & Opening Up. Jitri was only five years old at the time!

Liu Qing happily accepted the presidency of NICE. The Jiangsu Provincial Government sees JITRI as a test bed for research and development, and he felt that leading NICE would give him an opportunity to try something new. Also, he said with a twinkle in his eye and remembering his early irritation with the restrictions and regulations of government bureaucracy, "It would give me a chance to break some government rules and find a more efficient way to spend their funding money." Though this funding all comes from the Shanghai and Jiangsu governments, NICE is now expanding its activities into neighbouring Zhejiang and Anhui Provinces, and Liu Qing is actively cultivating similar tech research and development in many other regions of China – personally doing what he can to make a reality that China become a knowledge and innovation economy.

NICE and JITRI are really one public organisation, whose two administrative and managerial teams work as one team. Liu Qing is President of both, and he is also a Professor of Materials Science at Nanjing Tech.

NICE has several functions: to fund new tech startups; to encourage members of the Chinese diaspora with tech skills who have been living abroad to return to China by offering them research facilities and funding; to bridge the divide between university research and the tech skills needed by industry for greater innovation; and to modernise science and engineering education so that universities are producing more innovative students. At the present time, NICE employs 220 service staff in Shanghai and Nanjing and works with 100 universities, 300 industries, and 18,000 researchers working in 93 research institutes, each with 200 researchers. One of the organisational development stages currently being undertaken by NICE is the creation of an interactive and co-creative ecosystem that will connect and draw all elements of this vast research network into one, super-effective whole. An ecosystem similar to Haier's Quantum Management/RenDanHeYi model is envisaged.

Each of the 93 NICE research institutes is led by a Project Leader, and personnel to fill these posts are recruited from all over the world. But their readiness for this responsibility is another of the organisational development challenges still facing NICE. Being a Project Leader in such an organisation requires both technical and managerial skills. The people recruited do have very impressive tech backgrounds and skills, but few have the required management skills. Several of the funded startups have failed, for instance, because of things like inadequate market research. They may have been located in the wrong city or region, where consumer demand is weak, the products or systems they have developed may be ill suited to the needs of industry, or they may simply fail to market them well. Again, Liu Qing envisages training these Project Leaders in Quantum Management principles to improve management expertise. Quantum Management, for instance, advises companies to follow Haier's RenDanHeYi example and always get to know their customers and find out from them what they need *before* they start manufacturing their products. Quantum companies are always customer-led.

NICE research focuses on five areas: materials, biotech, energy and the environment, IT, and advanced manufacturing. NICE also has strategic partnerships with universities and research institutes located all over the world.

So far, it has funded 350 tech startups, and these have spawned a further 1200 startups, half of which are devoted to research and development, and the other half are companies making innovative products. One of their startups has become an IPO (listed company), and that has reaped them ten times their original funding investment.

China faces several challenges to becoming the Innovation Economy Liu Qing envisions, and the task of tackling many of these falls to NICE. Chinese research papers rank Number 1 globally, but innovation by Chinese industries lags far behind. Much of this stark difference follows from the wide divide between university research and industry, innovation, research, and development. Most universities in China function as islands unto themselves, with little or no knowledge or connection with industry, and thus prefer to concentrate on pure research that ignores practical application. Also, engineers working in industry have little knowledge of the relevant research being done at the universities. Then, too, the students being graduated from the universities do not possess the research skills and innovative talent needed by industry.

Students entering university are the products of a national school system focused entirely on their doing well on the very difficult *Gau Kao* exam that all Chinese students must take at the end of the final year of high school. This exam is the sole determining factor of whether a high school graduate will gain good employment opportunities or a place at a good university. From a very early age, under the watchful eye of demanding "tiger parents," and to the exclusion of all else – free time for exploration or reflection, social activities, friendships, community involvement, etc., students devote themselves to the passive absorption, and associated homework, of study material that will be covered on the *Gau Kao*. They arrive at university with no social or communication skills and no knowledge of self-exploration skills, expert only at passing an exam. Many don't even know what they want to do once at university, their sole purpose of all that hard study having been to *get into* "a good university." Then at university, there is more time- and energy-consuming passive learning devoted to passing more exams.

Graduate students at university are encouraged to focus on producing publications rather than on doing practical research, and those doing science or engineering subjects have no exposure to the humanities or the wider cultures of art, music, or poetry. Thus, university students arrive for research positions in industry having no social or communication skills, no practical experience of having been part of a research team, and wholly ignorant of the activities and needs of industry, their imaginations and innovative thinking skills stunted by years of narrow, passive learning, and their only skill knowing how to pass an exam. At present, 40% of graduate students who join companies leave their jobs within one year.

One way that NICE is addressing this problem is to take lessons from things like the Catapult Program in the UK and the Switching Program introduced by the University of Waterloo in Canada, whereby university science and engineering students spend part of each academic year doing their studies at university, and another part of each year working with practical research teams in industry, receiving academic credit for both. This requires joint supervision by both universities and industry. In addition, NICE is encouraging the universities to become more aware of the innovation needs of industry by introducing real problems of industry into university research programmes, and thus to have students doing more practically oriented research as part of their academic work. At cooperating universities, NICE is so far sponsoring 2500 students with scholarships to do this problem-oriented research. They hope this number can reach 10,000. The joint benefits of this are that universities get real projects that can lead to real products, and companies gain a link with universities and an opportunity to get to know the students. The students themselves benefit, of course, by getting real work and real-world experience.

NICE are also promoting the ideas of joint professorships between university and industry that combine one professor from the university and one from a company, and a wider education curriculum for engineering and science students that would incorporate some study of the humanities. Some of these measures resonate with the Quantum Management for School Governance principles that were introduced in Guandong Province by Li Ling (see Chapter 10), and Liu Qing thinks that other Quantum Management for Education principles might be promoted.

Another measure NICE has introduced to counter the innovation gap in student educational provision has been to found JITRI Tech, a month-long residential summer academy for materials science students based at JITRI's research facility in Suzhou. This is meant to deepen students' understanding of the structure and performance of materials used in industry by confronting them with such "meaning questions" as, "What is plastic? Why is metal hard? Why is plastic placed on the outside of an electric wire?" The students are also introduced to the pioneering ideas in materials science. And a second line of study has the students looking at questions like, "How do you define a problem? How can you use technology to solve your problem?" In addition, they are introduced to general business knowledge, how to run a company, what they should know about costs, customers, competition, and investors. And to broaden their general knowledge and critical thinking skills, the JITRI Tech students are encouraged to ask a lot of questions, to learn to question their own and others' assumptions, they are treated to lectures on things like Buddhism, Jewish culture and the argumentative style of Jewish Talmudic study, quantum philosophy and Quantum Management, they engage in dialogue and discussion groups to improve communication skills, and are taken on a day-trip to a special arts and crafts village nearby. During the summer programme of 2023, 60 third-year undergraduate and graduate students attended JITRI Tech, some of them assisted with scholarships, and it is hoped to expand student numbers in future years.

NICE is doing important work that will benefit China and, indeed, the whole world. Under the quantum leadership of Liu Qing, it is becoming a quantum organisation.

Conclusion
The Challenges & Opportunities of Quantum Management

I have tried to demonstrate in this book that Quantum Management is more than just a revolutionary new management paradigm. It is a new philosophy, embedded in a new worldview, a new way of experiencing life, ourselves, each other, and our place in the universe. Like quantum physics itself, Quantum Management challenges us to rethink *everything* we previously thought about reality, life, leadership, what it means to be human, and the nature, role, and meaning of companies. And like all great challenges, it offers us an opportunity to envision a better version of ourselves, of the world we make together, and the very important role that companies can play in making these a reality. These are challenges and opportunities for all, but some of them differ for the world's different cultures.

For the Chinese people, this book has demonstrated that a quantum way of thinking and doing things is very familiar. Quantum thinking is embedded in much of ancient Chinese thought and even in the structure and comprehension of the Chinese language. Quantum Management itself was first implemented by Haier, a Chinese company, and is now being adopted by many more Chinese companies as a modernised expression of Chinese management. But even for the Chinese, there are cultural challenges.

There have long been two quite contrasting strains of thought in the Chinese tradition. Both stress the alignment of Heaven, Man, and Earth, the role of human beings as the "bridge between Heaven and Earth," and thus the responsibility of humans to embed or mirror the Dao, or Way of the universe, in the things and relationships we build here on Earth. Both recognise the unity of all Being and beings and thus the duty of all people to serve and care for others as they would for members of their own family, and to engage in lifelong self-cultivation so that their lives bring maximum benefit to society. And both emphasise virtue and benevolence as necessary qualities of all who would aspire to leadership. But there is a considerable difference in the two strains of Chinese culture about how these are best realised and practised.

That line of the tradition rooted in much of Daoism and neo-Confucian philosophy, particularly the philosophy of Wang Yang Ming, emphasises the dynamic nature of reality and relationship, and hence of organisations,

Wu wei, or "light touch" leadership, the equality and importance of all people, the respect due to all, thus less hierarchy, the possible harm of "too much learning," i.e. over reliance on books and written authority for one's moral cultivation, and the importance of sincerity over mere practice of the rites. Wang Yang Ming, especially, stresses the moral authority and self-development of the individual person by writing about *Liangzhi*, each person's innate moral intuition and thus ability to determine right and wrong for themselves. He thus downplays the importance of authority and authority figures, even the unquestioned "authority of Heaven" (often, in the more authoritarian mainstream Confucianism, to mean the authority of the Emperor), ritual practice, and reliance on written texts, emphasising instead reflection, self-questioning, meditation, and thought in action as the vehicles of moral self-cultivation and the development and practice of virtue. He encourages questioning, critical thinking, and exploration. This is the strain of Chinese philosophical thought most close to the philosophy and practice of quantum leadership and Quantum Management. Both Lao Tzu and Wang Yang Ming are the favoured thinkers, along with the *I Ching* itself, frequently studied and referred to by the Chinese business leaders wanting to modernise Chinese management.

The other powerful strain of Chinese philosophical thought, one that still has a great influence on day-to-day Chinese culture and social attitudes, is mainstream Confucianism. Arising from the written commentaries and teachings of Confucius' disciples over hundreds, even thousands of years, and not always truly reflecting the thoughts of Confucius himself as expressed in the *Analects*, this strain of Chinese culture strongly emphasises social hierarchy, respect for and deference to elders and other figures of authority like national leaders, teachers, and workplace superiors, respect for and adherence to tradition, social rituals and customs. It discourages questioning, thinking for oneself, any challenge to authority, or the way "things are usually done," thus questioning and personal experimentation. It tends to give much of society a static nature and lies behind the exam-focused, passive learning still dominant in Chinese education, the reluctance of students to explore or ask questions, and the disappointing innovative spirit or talent of so many Chinese university graduates.

In contrast with those later desciples who sought to define "Confucianism" in his name, Confucius himself "asked lots of questions," counselled rulers to "seek and listen to many opinions" before making decisions, and respected talented craftsmen and competent junior officials to be trusted to get on with their work without supervision or instructions from him or any other authority figure. And, like Wang Yang Ming, Confucius believed that the people are more important than the authority figures who would supervise or rule over them.

Quantum Management philosophy and practice present a great challenge to the mainstream Confucian strain of Chinese culture. On the other hand, it offers a science-based opportunity in keeping with the traditional Chinese worldview, and much of China's greatest thought, for mainstream Chinese to follow a more innovative path towards modernising education, the management of organisations, education, and perhaps openness to more experimentation with relationships and social customs. Several Western commentators on Chinese history have suggested that many of China's dynasties in the past were short-lived because they suppressed dynamism and thus became static and rigid. The young entrepreneurs in China's tech startups, and those free to explore, experiment, and make "creative mistakes" in quantum companies like Haier, have certainly unleashed a palpably energetic dynamism that is felt and commented on by visitors to China. Were that same modernising spirit accepted more widely, this dynamism would permeate the whole of society.

Both the challenges posed to and the opportunities offered by Quantum Management philosophy and practice to those living in Western cultures are greater. The reason that Western people find quantum physics "counterintuitive" and "impossible to understand," so much of quantum philosophy alien, and that most Western companies have shown so little interest in adopting Quantum Management, is that quantum physics and the quantum worldview underpinning Quantum Management challenge the very foundations of Western thought, Western religion, and the whole, mainstream Western worldview. The West simply finds it difficult to *think* in a quantum way. The roots of Western culture and thinking lie in the very formal either/or logic of Aristotle and in the monotheism and beliefs of the Judeo/Christian religion. The resulting worldview, much of which is embedded in the Latin grammar underlying most Western languages, and in nearly all Western philosophy, separates the subject and the object and distinguishes the human observer and the world he/she observes, and thus values the superiority of objectivity and the separation of truth from relationship or context. Western religions similarly stress the absolute difference and separation of human beings from Heaven, or God, and of humans from Nature, and the singularity of Absolute Truth and "one best way."

All this then came to its ultimate expression and legitimacy as "scientific truth" in Newton's 17th-century mechanistic physics and then the near total dominance of a Newtonian worldview and its influence on every major Western thinker for the following three hundred years, including Frederick Taylor, the founder of the Scientific Management still practised by most Western companies. The Newtonian worldview, with its emphasis on the separation and isolation of atoms, the sole significance of a narrowly deterministic material reality, "one best way" and one Absolute Truth, then influenced the nature of Western medicine, with its focus on the body as a collection of separate parts, education, with its division of knowledge into learning siloes, the exaggerated, selfish individualism of "atomistic citizens," the corrosive selfish and narrowly materialist values of Western capitalism, and a Western arrogance that views the Western way as the one, best way. This arrogance makes it impossible for Western people to think there could be any intuition or logic different from their own, any culture or values other than their own worth considering, any way of doing things other than their own worth practising – "our way is the best way, the only valid way." All this, accompanied by an arrogance of power that typifies most Western business leadership, is of course challenged by the philosophy and practice of Quantum Management.

But just as the challenges posed to the West are great, so are the opportunities offered by becoming open to the quantum worldview. The same thinking, cultural features and preferences that make Quantum Management a challenge for the West also underpin the betrayal of its own democratic values and the social fracture that are feeding the right wing populist movements now tearing Western societies apart – wealth, power, and social inequality, intolerance of difference and racist bigotry, limited or non-existent access to housing, health care, and higher education, violence, loneliness, drug addiction, and resentment of a false meritocracy and elitism that favours the wealth and social privilege of a fortunate few. Adoption of the values, practices, and worldview inherent in the philosophy and practice of Quantum Management could offer healing to all this. And it would act to correct the reluctance of many Western nations to embrace the measures necessary to end the pollution and degradation of the environment that have caused climate change.

There is a further challenge of Quantum Management to all cultures and thought leaders around the world. I have shown evidence in this book that many Chinese companies are readily adopting Quantum Management because its philosophy and worldview find natural roots in traditional Chinese culture. Thus, many foreign visitors to Haier have commented, "I can see this works in China, but it would never work at home." Could these cultures other than China find a similar resonance with features of their own tradition? I believe that India, for instance, easily could. There is a natural affinity with much of quantum thought in India's Upanishads, its Vedanta tradition certainly, and in the leadership philosophy offered in its beloved *Bhagavad Gita*. The Sufi tradition of Islam and even many elements of more mainstream Koranic culture have resonances with the quantum worldview. Even in America, the nation's repressed and denied native American tradition has obvious resonance with the quantum worldview, as does the work of hitherto more marginalised Western philosophers like Spinoza, Hegel, and Heidegger, as well as Whitehead's philosophy and the work of Teilhard de Chardin. Could there be other adaptations in other nations and cultures? I am prone to believe so. If I am right, the opportunities for world business, and greater global harmony and cooperation among nations, are enormous.

Bibliography

Al-Khalil, Jim, and McFadden, Johnjoe, *Life on the Edge: The Coming Age of Quantum Biology*, Penguin Random House, New York, London: 2015.
Angle, Stephen, *Sagehood*, Oxford University Press, Oxford: 2009.
Arthur, W. Brian, *Complexity and the Economy*, Oxford University Press, Oxford: 2014.
Brook, Peter, *The Empty Space*, Penguin, New York, London: 1968.
Brown, B.H., *The Wisdom of the Chinese*, Brentano's, Norwood, MA: 1920. Reprinted by University of Michigan Library.
Cau, Antonio S., Editor, *Encyclopedia of Chinese Philosophy*, Routledge, New York, London: 2003.
Collins, James C., "Level-5 Leadership," *Harvard Business Review*, July-August, 2005.
Confucius, *The Analects*, translated by David Hinton, Counterpoint, Berkeley: 2014.
Fang, Thome H., *The Chinese View of Life*, Linking Publishing Co., Ltd, Taipei: 1980.
Gardener, Daniel K., translator, *The Four Books: The Basic Teachings of the Later Confucian Tradition*, Hackett Publishing Company, Inc., Indianapolis, Cambridge: 2007.
Hadamard, J., *Essay on the Psychology of Invention in the Mathematical Field*, Princeton University Press, Princeton: 1945.
Hinton, David, *China Roots: Taoism, Ch'an, and Original Zen*, Shambala Press, Boulder, CO: 2020.
Hinton, David, translator, *Tao Te Ching*, Counterpoint, Berkeley, CA: 2015.
Huang, Alfred, *The Complete I Ching, Inner Traditions*, Rochester, Vermont, Toronto: 1998.
Hui, Yuk, *The Question Concerning Technology in China: An Essay in Cosmotechnics*, Urbanomic Media, Falmouth: 2016.
Janni, Nicholas, *Leader as Healer*, LID, London, New York, etc.: 2022.
Jaworski, Joseph, *Synchronicity*, Berrett-Koehler, San Francisco, CA: 1996.
Jullien, Francois, *From Being to Living*, Sage, Los Angeles, London, etc.: 2020.
Jullien, Francois, *The Propensity of Things*, Zone Books, New York: 1999.
Lau, D.C., translator, *Confucius: The Analects*, Penguin Books, London, New York, etc.: 1979.
Lau, D.C., translator, *Mencius*, Penguin Books, London, New York, etc.: 1970, 2003.
Losada, Marcial, "Caring", abridgement and translation of Umberto Maturan's "Student's Prayer", unpublished.

McGilchrist, Iain, *The Matter with Things*, Two Volumes, Persperctiva Press, London: 2021.
Mo Tzu, *The Mozi: The Ethical and Political Works of Mo Tzu*, R. Medeiros, Editor, Y. Merei, translator, Amazon Kindle: April 2021.
Prigogine, Ilya, and Stengers, Isabelle, *Order Out of Chaos: Man's New Dialogue with Nature*, Bantam, New York: 1984.
Shannon, Benny, and Atlan, Henri, "Von Foerster's Theorem on Connectedness and Organization: Semantic Applications," *New Ideas in Psychology*, Vol. 8, No. 1, pp. 81–90: 1990.
Sun, Tzu, *The Art of War*, translated by Gary Gagliardfi, Science of Strategy Institute/ Clearbridge, Seattle: 1999.
Tu, Wei-Ming, *Confucian Thought*, State University of New York Press, Albany: 1990.
Wang Yangming, *Instructions for Living and Other Writings*, translated by Wing-tsit Chan, Columbia University Press, New York & London: 1963.
Waters, Geoffry, Farman, Michael, and Lunde, David, translators, *300 Tang Poems*, White Pines Press, Buffalo, New York: 2011.
West, Geoffrey, *Stages*, Widenfeld & Nicholson, London: 2017.
Wilhelm, Richard, translator, *I Ching*, Penguin Books, London: 1983.
Zhang, Zai, *The Western Inscription*, Cheng Meng, Hong Kong: 1983.
Zhang, Zai, in Cau, Antonio S., Editor, *The Encyclopedia of Chinese Philosophy*, Routledge, New York & London: 2003.
Zohar, Danah, *The Quantum Self*, Bloomsbury, London: 1990.
Zohar, Danah, *The Quantum Society*, Bloomsbury, London: 1994.
Zohar, Danah, *The Quantum Leader*, Prometheus, Amherst, MA: 2016.
Zohar, Danah, *Zero Distance*, Palgrave MacMillan, Singapore: 2022.
Zohar, Danah, *Through the Time Barrier*, Heinemann, London: 1982.

Index

Analects of Confucius 62, 65, 81, 117
ancient Chinese 24, 116
Angle, Stephen 61
Arthur, Brian 25
The Art of War (Sun Tzu) 1, 15, 68, 76, 87
associative thinking 45–47; *see also* "thinking"

A Ballad of Peach Blossom Spring (Wang Wei) 23
Bezerra, Lara 32
Bhagavad Gita 119
Bible 13, 34
biochemical and biophysical processes 64
Bohm, David 3, 14, 16, 18, 31, 47, 50, 51; "Separation is an illusion" 19; thinking about quantum physics 4; work 8
Bohr, Niels 21; Principle of Complementarity 3
bosons 69, 94
British energy leaders 11; *see also* leaders
Brook, Peter 29
business-as-usual management practices 49
"business-as-usual" paradigm 27, 49, 70; *see also* paradigms

CADs *see* complex adaptive systems (CADs)
celebrate diversity 109–110
Chan (Zen) Buddhism 2, 29, 81, 82; practice 65; tradition 67
Chardin, Teilhard de 119
Chen Feng 37–39
Cheng Yi 72

China/Chinese: acupuncture 16; ancient philosophers 2; ancient thinkers 109; art and calligraphy 29; business community 37; civil war 98; classics of 2, 3, 16; companies 7, 31, 116; contribution 3; culture 5, 16, 66, 110, 116, 117; Daoist 6; dragons 16–17; great philosophers 56; great thinkers 17, 57; *I Ching* 3, 4, 11, 15, 17, 20–21, 23, 29, 33, 38, 51, 56, 59, 62, 68, 73, 74, 81, 111, 117; knowledge & innovation economy 111–115; language 15, 59, 98, 116; management 4; medicine 30; military strategy 18; model 5; National Innovation Center 108; natural systems thinkers 19; notion of ideal leader 56; paintings 17; parliament 111; people 76; philosophers 40, 58, 61, 65; philosophical thought 117; philosophy 2, 6, 24; poetry 15; quantum leaders *see* China's quantum leaders; and quantum systems 5; sages 67, 73; thinkers 62; thought 61, 67; tradition 20, 33, 58, 63, 64, 66, 75, 82, 109; worldview 13; *yin/yang* polarity 20, 34; Zhou Dynasty 1
China's quantum leaders: Haier's *RenDanHeyi* Management Model 2, 7, 27, 30, 67, 81–85, 87–97, 108; Li Ling 102–110, 115; Liu Qing 111–115; Zhang Ruimin 2, 7, 27, 55, 81–91, 93, 97; Zhu Haibin (Eagle Zhu) 98–101
Chuang Tzu 33
"closed systems" 28
companies: Chinese 7, 31, 116; dynamic company system 27; quantum 18–19, 21, 26–32, 61, 65, 67; Quantum

124 Index

Management in 7; traditional Taylorian companies 44; *see also* Haier
compassion 74–75
complex adaptive systems (CADs) 12, 25–32, 42, 47, 63–67, 70–72, 75, 76, 91, 109
complexity science 4, 7, 12, 24–26, 28, 63, 81, 88
Confucianism 2, 5, 17, 29, 117
Confucius/Confucian 1, 2, 4, 5, 14, 20, 37, 58, 60, 68, 70, 71, 73–75; *Analects* 62, 65, 81, 85, 117; culture 76; sage-king 57; thought 51, 110; tradition 56, 57; values 76
contemporary model, for scientific management 13
"cosmic consciousness" 51–52
cultivating quantum thinking 48–50; *see also* "thinking"
Cultural Revolution 82
"curious behaviour," of quantum micro-world 3

Dahan Group in China 31; *see also* companies
Dao de Ching 58, 64, 66, 75, 84–87, 116
Daoism/Daoist 2–3, 6, 17, 29, 81, 86, 94, 95, 98, 101, 116; *see also* holism
Dao te Ching 98
Dayawa Experimental School 104–106, 108
Deng Xiao Ping: "Great Reform and Opening Up" initiative 112
Doctrine of the Mean 13, 72
Drucker, Peter 90
Duke Zhou 73
dynamic company system 27
dynamic polarity 20–22

Eagle Zhu *see* Zhu Haibin (Eagle Zhu)
East Asian cultures 43
ecosystems 6, 19, 21, 30, 69, 71, 83–86, 96, 97, 109, 113
"edge of chaos" 27–28, 61
"extraneous" information 49

Fang, Thome (Fang Dongmei) 34
Feynman, Richard 4
Five Movements/Five Elements 14
"fuzzy assessment" 107

ganying 51, 52
Gau Kao 114
Goethe, Johann Wolfgang: *Sorrows of Young Werther* 24
Great Absence 15, 18
Great Emptiness 13, 14
The Great Learning (Zhu Xi) 58, 60, 61, 64, 69, 76, 87
group project-based learning 102
guanxi 18

Haier 2, 7, 27, 30, 69; Ecosystem Brand 83, 92, 96–97; *RenDanHeyi* Management Model 2, 7, 27, 30, 67, 81–85, 87–97, 108; Zhang Ruimin (CEO) 2, 7, 27, 55, 81–91, 93, 97; *see also* companies
"At Haier, everyone is a thinker" (motto) 27
Hamel, Gary 90, 95
Harvard Business Review 73
Hegel, Georg Wilhelm Friedrich 119
Heisenberg, Werner 1, 2, 5, 119; thinking 3; Uncertainty Principle 3, 12, 17, 29, 59, 70
Heraclitus 84, 85
Hinton, David 5
holism/holistic 6, 19–20, 25, 28, 30–31, 67–69, 91, 96, 109; *see also* Daoism
humility 5, 73–74, 76, 81

I Ching 3, 4, 11, 15, 17, 20, 21, 23, 29, 33, 38, 51, 56, 59, 62, 68, 73, 74, 81, 111, 117
"If it works, don't fix it" (motto) 95
immutable Laws of Nature 44
Inamori, Kazuo: *A Compass to Fulfillment* 108; *Respect the Divine and Love People* 108
Indian *Upanishads* 58
"integration nodes" 93
Internet of Things (IoT) 81, 85, 86, 88, 90

Jiang Jeh Min 112
Jiangsu Industrial Technology Research Institute (JITRI) 112, 113, 115
Jung, Karl 51

Koranic culture 119
Kuang Chung-chi 36

Lao Tzu 1, 2, 4, 5, 8, 13, 57, 73, 85, 86, 110, 117; *Dao de Ching* 84; principle of *wu wei* 109
leaders: British energy 11; Chinese notion of 56; quantum 16, 17, 33, 37, 38, 42, 55–62
leadership: new paradigm 1–8; quantum *see* quantum leadership; quantum physics 1, 6; sage-king 55–62; Western business 119; Western-style top-down 27; *wu wei* 4, 99, 102, 109, 117; *see also* leader
level of system coordination 93
liangzi 51, 52, 58, 117
Li Keqiang 82
Li Ling 102–110, 115
Liu Qing 111–115
living quantum systems *see* complex adaptive systems (CADs)
logic-defying mysteries 3
Lovelock, James: Gaia hypothesis 25

machine-like serial thinking 45; *see also* "thinking"
Mach's principle 19; *see also* principles
Mandate of Heaven 40
man-made organisations 43
Mencius 4, 33, 57, 65, 71–73, 76
"messiness" 27, 28
microenterprises (MEs) 27, 67, 72, 73, 86, 91–97
Modernised Chinese Management Model 81
modern science 4, 42, 88
Mo Tzu 74

National Innovation Center (NICE) 108, 111–115
nature 23, 51; all-encompassing order of 24; CADs 63; and cosmos 12; and evolution process 109; humans from 118; immutable Laws of 44; living systems 64; and process of evolution 109; rule of 99; rule of Heaven 99; and universe 48
neo-Confucian philosophy 116
networked thinking 45–47; *see also* "thinking"
neural networks 45–48
neural tracts 43–45
new leadership paradigm 1–8; *see also* paradigms

new scientific paradigm 7; *see also* paradigms
Newtonian worldview 118
Newton, Isaac: paradigm of 43, 44; physics 17, 18, 26, 34; 17th-century mechanistic physics 12; structure 90–97
NICE *see* National Innovation Center (NICE)
Nolan, Kevin 89

"Observer Effect," in quantum theory 3
"open systems" 28
organisations: man-made organisations 43; principles 22, 31; quantum 71–73

paradigms: "business-as-usual" 27, 49, 70; leadership 1–8; new scientific 7; Newton, Isaac 43, 44; quantum 42, 43; Quantum Management 33; quantum physics 7
Pauli, Wolfgang 3, 16
Penrose, Roger 47, 51
philosophy: Chinese 2, 6, 24; neo-Confucian 116; of Quantum Management 6, 117–119; quantum physics 2, 7
Prigogine, Ilya 28
principles: Bohr's Principle of Complementarity 3; Heisenberg's Uncertainty Principle 3, 12, 17, 29, 59, 70; Lao Tzu's *wu wei* 109; Mach's principle 19; organisational principles 22, 31; of Quantum Management 6, 7, 13, 98, 104; Quantum Management for Education 115; Quantum Management for School Governance 115; of quantum physics 8, 51; twelve principles of quantum leadership 63–77; universal, of transformation 63

quantum: biology 7, 12, 47, 72; bits 69; companies 18–19, 21, 26–32, 61, 65, 67; cosmology 14; leadership *see* quantum leadership; morality 58; non-locality 52; organisations 71–73; paradigm 42, 43; physics *see* quantum physics; Quantum Management *see* Quantum Management; resonance 51, 52; schools 109–110; science 13, 18, 76; self 18, 58, 61, 75, 84; societies 61;

systems 71, 72, 91; technologies 26, 90; theory 3, 4; thinking 42, 47–48, 62, 116; universe 65, 72, 95; vacuum 14, 15, 33, 35, 68, 87; wave/particle duality 21
quantum leaders 16, 17, 33, 37, 38, 42; China *see* China's quantum leaders; as modern sage king 55–62
quantum leadership: essential foundation of 61; qualities of 48, 57; Quantum Management and 1, 6, 117; and quantum thinking 56; twelve principles of 63–77
Quantum Management 1, 2, 4–6, 13, 25, 26, 29, 31, 42, 56, 60, 66, 76, 108; benefits of 21; challenges & opportunities of 116–119; in companies 7; for education 109; for Education principles 115; essential characteristic of 19, 106; model 90; new paradigm 33; "no borders" 18; organisational principles by 22; philosophy and practice of 6, 117–119; practices 7; principles of 6, 7, 13, 98, 104; quantum leadership and 117; for School Governance 108; for School Governance principles 115; for schools 102–110; systems thinking and 20; workshop 11; *wuwei* 101
Quantum Management Theory 4, 6, 57, 63, 66, 81, 83, 84
quantum physics 2–7, 12, 14, 17, 18, 20–21, 25, 29, 31, 34, 47, 50, 67; discoveries of 42; field theory 4, 7; leadership 1, 6; logic 4; micro-world, "curious behaviour" of 3; modern expression in 81; non-locality 3; observer and observed revealed by 36; paradigm 7; philosophy 2, 7; principles of 8, 51; reality 4; science 2, 7; technologies 7; thinking 4–6; "wave/particle duality" 3; Western people "make sense" of 4
quirky effect 21

reframing 71–72, 74
RenDanHeyi management model 2, 7, 27, 30, 67, 81–85, 87–97, 108, 113
revolutionary quantum physics, 20th century 3
Rilke, Rainer Marie 35

sage-king leadership 55–62; *see also* leadership
Scientific American (Vendral) 8
scientific management 12, 13, 118
self-organising systems 26, 36, 109
sense of vocation/purpose 75–77
serial thinking 43–45; *see also* "thinking"
shanshui 23
Sorrows of Young Werther (Goethe) 24
Spinoza 3, 119
Stages (West) 24
Stanford Performance-based Assessment 107
Stone, Andrew 27, 35–36
Sufi tradition of Islam 119
Sun Tzu 19, 67; *The Art of War* 1, 15, 68, 76, 87

tacit knowledge/learning 46, 47
Tai Ch'i 16
Taixu 13
Tao te Ching 13–15, 17, 18, 20, 21, 23, 26, 63, 81, 82, 109
Taylor, Frederick 13, 118; "Scientific Management" 12; structure 90–97
"thinking" 43; associative thinking 45–47; cultivating quantum thinking 48–50; modernised Chinese management and 4, 6; networked thinking 45–47; "quantum" thinking 47–48; serial thinking 43–45
Third Reform 112
Tian Jian Water 37, 38
Tian Ren Heyi (Taoist mantra) 51, 63, 89
token of recognition 3
traditional: Chinese *see* traditional Chinese; management practices 11, 31; Taylorian companies 44; Western view 24
traditional Chinese 4, 31; management 5; paintings 15; philosophy, knowledge of 7; wisdom and modern science 88; wisdom and philosophy 81
Traditional Chinese Medicine 105, 108
trial-and-error learning 46
Tseng Tzu 65
Tu Wei-Ming 40
twelve principles, of quantum leadership 63–77
21st-century life, challenges and opportunities of 42

Uncertainty Principle (Heisenberg) 3, 12, 17, 29–30, 59, 70; *see also* principles
universal principles of transformation 63

Vendral, Vlatko: *Scientific American* 8
vocation/purpose, sense of 75–77
Von Foerster's Theorem 28

Wang Bi 24
Wang Fuzhi 15
Wang Wei: *A Ballad of Peach Blossom Spring* 23
Wang Yang Ming 5, 17, 51, 59, 66, 67, 71–73, 76, 81, 85, 95, 116–117; *Inquiry on the Great Learning* 64; *liangzu* 4, 58
Wan Se Bee Park ("Colorful Bee Park") 99–101
Weber, Max 28
Western: business leadership 119; capitalism 118; commentators on Chinese history 118; culture *see* Western culture; ideas 24; intuition 3; logic 3, 5, 20, 34, 43; management 11, 26; medicine 118; quantum physics 6; thinking 108

Western culture 45; for rethinking 7; and thinking 118
Western-style top-down leadership 27
West, Geoffrey 25; *Stages* 24
Whitehead, Alfred North 3, 119
Wu Nianbo 81
wu wei 4, 99, 102, 109, 117
wu zhi 66

Xunzi 65, 66

Yao Yeh 111
yin/yang-like dynamic polarity 3, 14, 20, 21, 34

Zero Distance (2021) 108
"Zero-Distance Model" 75, 90, 93, 106
Zhang Ruimin 2, 7, 27, 55, 81–91, 93, 97
Zhang Zai 4, 14, 16, 17, 20, 33, 51, 63, 68, 70, 74, 76
Zhangzu 4, 5
Zhongyong 72
Zhou Dunyi 57
Zhu Haibin (Eagle Zhu) 98–101
Zhu Minhao 98, 100
Zhu Xi 18, 58, 70, 86; *The Great Learning* 58, 60, 61, 64, 69, 76, 87

For Product Safety Concerns and Information please contact our EU representative GPSR@taylorandfrancis.com
Taylor & Francis Verlag GmbH, Kaufingerstraße 24, 80331 München, Germany

www.ingramcontent.com/pod-product-compliance
Lightning Source LLC
Chambersburg PA
CBHW052026290426
44112CB00014B/2390